THE CONJUR...

WORKING THE ROOT

STARR CASAS

THE CONJURE WORKBOOK
VOLUME I

WORKING THE ROOT

STARR CASAS

PENDRAIG Publishing
Los Angeles, CA 91040

The Conjure Workbook Volume I Working the Root
by Starr Casas
First Edition © 2013
by PENDRAIG Publishing
All rights reserved.

Cover Design & Interior Images
Typeset & Layout   Jo-Ann Byers Mierzwicki

PENDRAIG

PENDRAIG Publishing
Los Angeles, CA 91040
www.PendraigPublishing.com
Printed in the United States of America

ISBN: 978-1-936922-56-7

DEDICATION

This book is dedicated to my Ancestors.
Thanks Aunt Cora!

TABLE OF CONTENTS

FOREWORD

Dear Reader of the "Conjure Work Book",

It has been a mixed bag of joy and concern as I have watched the increasing interest in Southern Folk Magic become a "movement". The joy, is that finally America is a taking pride in one of its many old folk magic practices and its offerings to the world of magic and spirit. The concern is that while more and more information is available; less and less of the heart and soul of what galvanized and preserved the core of conjure is being presented.

The American South has produced many practices such as root-work, hoodoo, and conjure and they have a treasure trove of wisdom and power to offer. But, all of them originate in the struggle and strength of the conflicting political and cultural forces of the south. This included the forced displacement of Native Americans, slavery, poverty and civil war. Out of this has grown practices and traditions that reflect deep reflection, liberation of the soul and a relationship with the spirit world rooted in ancestral guidance and reverence. Without the voice of soul, the practices are shallow shells of nostalgia. With it, they are liberating forces of soul and spirit.

The Conjure Work Book is a literary soulful voice calling us back to the "root" and "spirit" of conjure. It is Mama Starr offering the reader roots and work that is traditional, healing and powerful!. This book is nuts-and-bolts, power-and prayer, heart-and-soul of conjure and root work. It provides spiritual voltage to the wiring of the recipes that are available to seeker of the ways of conjure and root work. I love Starr! I love her work! I love the way she truly and heartfully offers the teachings of her elders. I love the Conjure Workbook. I advise all workers to have it in the "must-have" section of their library.

Orion Foxwood

Orion is a conjurer in the southern folk tradition, a traditional witch and a faery seer. He is the founder of Foxwood Temple and the House of Brigh Faery Seership Institute; and a co-founder of Conjure Crossroads, the annual Folk Magic Festival in New Orleans, Conjure-Con in Santa Cruz, CA and 2Hoddos.com. He is the author of three books, The Faery Teachings, The Tree of Enchantment and The Candle and the Crossroads. He can be contacted at Orionfoxwood.com.

WARNING

Any reader who uses the works within this book
does so **entirely at their own risk.**

The author and publisher accept no liability
if the works do not have the desired effect
or if adverse affects are caused.

This book is **not** suitable for children.

This is my reading table where I do all my consultations

INTRODUCTION

This book started a long time ago. I had it in my mind to write a Conjure workbook; one that would touch on all areas of the work. My *"Hoodoo Money Conjure"* book came from the very first workbook I started; so did all the other books I have written. They all began in that workbook except for the *"Candle Burning Book"* that book started out as a booklet for a class I was giving at the *"Folk Magic Festival"* in NOLA. Before we go any further in this writing I want to say something. Well actually a few things. I by no means am an authority on Conjure work. I am just a plain ole worker! God has blessed me to be able to put my words on paper and to teach in order to help others learn. There are many other gifted, teachers, writers and workers out there. I've learned how to do the work from family, old folks I've met along the way and from my own ability to understand the work. There are others who have also been taught by folks they have met or by family members. They may teach or work a little different than I do but it is basically all the same work. It really just depends on what area you come from. Don't ever fall into the trap of thinking that one person has all the answers; they don't, myself included. Remember to expect to see folks who work different than you do or how you were taught. If we all worked the same there would be nothing to learn.

If you gathered fifteen workers in a room and gave them a work to do, I promise you none of them would do the work the same. Why; because we all come from different parts of the country and we all learned the work from different folks. Then on top of all that we have added our own style to the work. We could all learn something new from each other if we sat down and talked for a while together. The best way to learn is to keep an opened mind, talk to as many elders as you can. Old folks are a fountain of information if you just take the time to listen to what they have to say. A lot of information is hidden in the stories they have to tell; you just have to listen. They are not gonna just sit down and start spewing out remedies that is a misconception. It may take months for them to tell you anything but it is worth the wait. I have always been drawn to my elders, I guess that's why I have been so blessed with the knowledge I have.

When it's all said and done I'm just a RootWoman plain and simple. I first became acquainted with candle burning and incense when I was around fourteen and snuck off to go to the Catholic Church with my aunt. I may have been a little older; it's been a long time ago. My mama had a hissy fit over it. The year I turn seventeen three things happen that set me on my life's course. I became a Catholic, I had my first child, and I learned how to work with eggs and candles to heal. That was forty years ago. I've been learning and working ever since. When I was growing up my mama treated us but I didn't know what she was doing was called "Hoodoo". I never heard it called anything but work. I learned it was called "Hoodoo" when I got on the internet. It had been something that was part of my family's everyday life. It was just the way things were done in our home. We used to say it was "just mama's funny ways". One of the things that sticks out in my mind is that when we came into the house we had to take our shoe's off at the door; mama cleaned the bottom of our shoes then we took them to our room. Other mama's didn't do that and I always thought it was odd growing up until I understood what she was doing. We couldn't track tricks into the house if it stopped at the door. Its little things like this that make up Conjure; their everyday lives for folks who have grown up with Conjure.

Conjure or Hoodoo as it is known due to the internet is not a religion per say but it is strongly woven with-in Christianity and the Bible. Some folks don't agree with this which is their right, but every elder that has taught me has been a Christian; they can't all be wrong. Conjure focuses on making one's life better through prayer; it focuses on the home and hearth; Helping one in everyday living. The main concern of Conjure workers is blessing their homes and keeping the home peaceful; making sure their mate is faithful, drawing luck and much more. The way a rootworker achieves these things is by laying tricks or working the root. This is done through prayers, candles, lucky hands and other things; also a large amount of oils, powders and waters are used, along with different Salts. There are many works that have been incorporated into the daily lives of families, which have been handed down orally through the ages; from the way they sweep to the way their food is prepared. Like many other types of folk magic, Conjure attributes magical properties to herbs, roots, minerals, animal parts, and personal items. Although each generation adds its own twist to the work; the heart of the work remains the same, a living testimony to the beliefs of those who came before us.

Conjure or Hoodoo as it is sometimes called does not require a lot of elaborate preparation, expensive tools, or specialized knowledge. It also does not demand years of training in order to be successful. The most important tool you need is your Bible and faith in yourself that you can achieve your goal. Not I think it will; but I KNOW it will. Some people view this type of Magic as nothing more than superstition, or the ancient remnants of an unenlightened past. To those folks I say, "Don't knock it until you have tried it." To understand this type of magic you have to have an understanding of our ancestors who practiced it. If it seems too simple to be real; well you have to understand these were simple down-to-earth people. They worked from daylight until dark; by the time the end of the day came, they were too tired to do an elaborate ritual.

Rootwork was practiced in their everyday life from the way they swept their yards to the way they threw out old dishwater. They incorporated rootwork into their lives; it was an everyday practice for them. So don't be fooled by the simplicity of this type of magic. It does not take hours of ritual work and preparation to make this type of magic work. It is my hope that within these pages you will find useful information that will be easy to understand and will help you in the betterment of your life's goals. There are many simple and easy works within this book to achieve what you deem necessary to have fulfillment in your life.

ANCESTORS

First and foremost I'd like to say that honoring your dead is not worshipping them. The serving of our ancestor's is not a religion in and of itself, but a part of religious expression; the basis of serving our ancestor's stem from the belief that the spirits of the dead continue to dwell in the natural world and have the power to influence the fortune and fate of the living. It is also believed ancestors can assert their powers by blessing or cursing. They are also regarded as the intermediaries between the living and the divine powers. In general, ancestors are believed to wield great authority, having special powers to influence the course of events or to control the well being of their living relatives. Protection of the family is one of their main concerns. The serving of our ancestors consist of the lighting of candles, prayers, presenting gifts, and making offerings. In my family we honor our dead by cleaning and dressing their graves for holidays. They can and will remove all obstacles that maybe in your path. All you have to do is call upon them to come to your aid.

The serving of ancestor's has been found in various parts of the world. All societies give ritual attention to death or to the souls of the dead, but not all of these practices are called serving our ancestors. Our elders are always regarded with respect, and we continue to have a bond with them even though they have passed on. We still love them, we feel joy when we think of them, and we miss them. The bond was not severed when they pasted on because we have our memories of them. The spirits see, hear, feel, understand, and communicate with the living; they make moral judgments; they are wishful, willful, joyful, angry, stern, permissive, kind, and cruel, they have all the other emotions and traits of human beings. If your ancestor was a loving person when they when they walked among the living they still hold that trait, if they were cruel and heartless those emotions will still be there. Just because they have passed on doesn't mean they have changed their ways. That's why it is important that you call on the ancestors you know who loved you and will be happy to help you with your needs.

Before you call on your ancestors you need to say your prayers for protection. This is very important. If you don't know how to do this then you can call on your guardian angel to protect you. We all have a guardian angel we were given at birth. If you look in the Bible in the Book of Exodus and read *Exodus 23 V20-23* it say's:

> 20 *"Behold, I send an Angel before you to keep you in the way and to bring you into the place which I have prepared.*
>
> 21 *Beware of Him and obey His voice; do not provoke Him, for He will not pardon your transgressions; for My name is in Him.*
>
> 22 *But if you indeed obey His voice and do all that I speak, then I will be an enemy to your enemies and an adversary to your adversaries.*
>
> 23 *For My Angel will go before you and bring you in to the Amorites and the Hittites and the Perizzites and the Canaanites and the Hivites and the Jebusites; and I will cut them off.*

When you have finished your prayers then you can call on your ancestors. I was told as a young worker that it is always good to remind them that you belong to them. Here is an example of how I call my ancestors; I'll say:

> *I so and so call on my ancestors, blood of my blood; I call on those of my ancestors who are*

willing to come to my aid and help me. I call on those who have loved me in life and death; also those who are known and those who are unknown to me.

Below is the prayer I use for my ancestors.

PRAYER

Blessings, to all my departed ancestors; Particular blessings and thankfulness to {repeat the names 3 times}, as well as all those whose names I do not know but whose blood runs through my veins.

Please accept the coolness of this water so that you may be cool and comfortable. Please accept the light and energy so that you may have brightness and strength. I love and miss your presence here on Earth but gather strength and wisdom from your continued energy and guidance.

May that guidance continue to open my paths and roads and the paths and roads of those I love. May your wisdom bring love and prosperity into my home. May you place a wall of protection around me and those I love; that no harm or anything negative will be able to breach.

After you have lit a vigil and said your prayers you can ask your ancestors to assist you in any work you need to do. Some workers will say that you should never ask your ancestor to help you with work. I was taught that your ancestors will help you when no other spirit will. They want us to achieve our goal; they are there to help make our life better. They will be more than happy to help you. You need to feed your ancestors at least once a week. I do this every Monday morning. I give them a light, fresh cool water and prayers. Place their offerings on their space light their vigil then you will knock three times, and call on your ancestors. Give them your prayers and blessings, if you have offerings to give them bring them to their attention at this time. If you need their help now is the time to ask for it. Remember your altar is a holy place and it is important that you keep it clean and treat it as such. You must always treat it and the spirits with respect. Also remember not to only go to them when you need to petition them for help; set up a day of the week and honor them weather you need their help or not. If you just call on them when you need something they will feel used.

If you can you should go to your altar everyday at least for five minutes, if you do this you will become stronger in your work. I know it's hard in this day and time to have the time to do the things we need but where your spiritual life is concerned you just have to make time.

Ancestor Altar

If you are interested in making your own ancestor altar here are some instruction's that will help. I want to point out first that this is a very important step. Do not take this lightly; it is a great responsibility you are taking upon yourself. You can't just put an altar together and throw a few things on it. This space has to be cleansed and treated as you would any Holy place. You will find more information in the section of the book labeled "Altars". It is your responsibility to keep the altar clean, to feed your ancestors, and offer them candles, prayers and other offerings. If you cannot do this then please don't set up an altar until a time when you will be able to tend to the altar, as it should be taken care of.

There are two rules that you need to follow; never place Salt or a picture of a living person on your ancestor altar. The spirits will not come around where there is Salt and you should never place the living among the dead. The ole folks will tell you that if you place the living among those who have passed it makes our ancestors hunger to be with the living. It could cause an early death for a loved one. Other than having a white cloth and some water in glasses on your altar you can place whatever you want to on the altar. Here are a few ideas for your altar. You can place, flowers, a cross, picture's of your loved ones who have passed, things that your ancestors liked to have around them, dirt from a place they liked to visit or a little of their graveyard dirt can be placed in a nice bowl on the altar; the list can go on and on. Always do what feels right to you. If you follow your heart you can't go wrong.

ALTARS

When you decide to set up an altar the first thing you need to do is to decide where you are going to place the altar. I personally would not place it where I sleep. When you sleep you are defenseless, burning candles brings the spirits into an area. Now this is just me; I have burned candles beside my bed but it was for a different reason altogether. Some of you may disagree with me and that's ok too.

An altar is a holy space for you to be able to do your work. The altar can be set up on a table or the floor. Putting together an altar is very personal so it really depends on you and the spirit you are going to be working with as to where you place your altar. As far as I am concerned there are no fast hard rules for setting up an altar. I have a few set rules for myself as far as my altars go. My ancestor altar will always face the East so that the sun will always rises in front of them; the other one is that

This is my families New Years altar.

my money altar is never placed in the West where the sun goes down. I want to make money not lose money. Other than these two rules that I have set for myself to follow there are no rules.

I have a few different altars and they are all set up differently depending on the spirit or the Saint they are made for. Most of the time the spirit will lead you in the direction you should go when you are going to put up an altar; most spirits have their own colors and items that they prefer on their altars. Blackhawk likes to be placed in a bucket or a tub as you can see in the picture. All his tools are kept with him and the work is done within his tub. The more you work within the tub or bucket the more powerful it will become; after all you are filling it full of power with all your prayers and petitions.

This next altar is of La Madama (Mammy or Aunt Jemima) altar. Out of honor and respect I call her La Madama; I refuse to call her Mammy! La Madama was a slave in real life. She is the one that ran the house, she doctored all the ills and made sure everyone was taken care of. I was taught she was a rootwoman, that she collected roots and herbs, she made remedies to heal the sick in the house and she also had the gift of sight. She

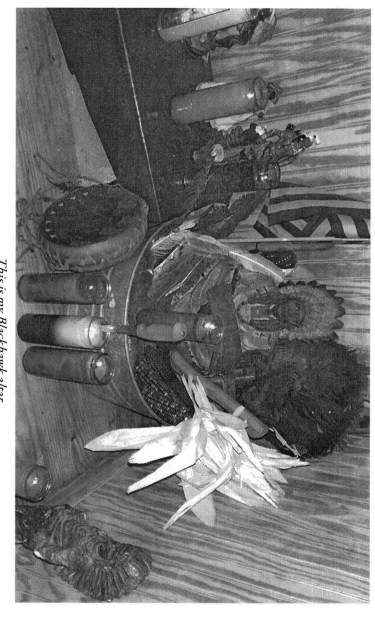

This is my Blackhawk altar.

protected and took care of her family. As you can see from the picture her home is within an iron pot.

Within her pot are all of her tools that she works with. La Madama can help you with all areas of your life, she is very helpful to readers and she will help you see clearly. If you are having a problem within your family or with your spouse she fix that situation fast and in a hurry. I have seen her do the job within thirty minutes. If she chooses to work with you she will be there for you anytime you call on her.

This last altar belongs to my beloved St. Martha the Dominator. I have worked with her for many, many years. She is very powerful when it comes to any type of male dominance work or enemy work. She will work within minutes of being petitioned. I have seen her work miracles. Her main colors are green and purple. If you are having problems with your husband then she is the one to petition.

As you can see from my photo's each one of these altars are very different. They each service very different spirits and they each have a different feel to them. No one can tell you what is right or wrong for you to place on your altar; that is very personal and completely up to you and the spirit the altar belongs to. If you listen closely the spirit will guide you on the way they want their space to be set up, all you have to do is listen. You do how ever have to prepare your space before you set your altar up. You will cleanse and bless your area.

Once you figure out where you will place your altar you need to sweep the wall down from top to bottom. And sweep the area where the altar will sit. You then need to make a wash of about one cap of ammonia and a splash of Florida water. Wash the wall from top to bottom and mop the floor as well. Pray *Psalm 23* while you are cleaning your area. Wipe down the table you will set your altar on with this wash. Once you have done this you are ready to set up your altar. One thing that every altar needs is a cloth, a glass of water and a vigil burning on it. Anything else

you decide to add is up to you and the spirit you are working with. Within this workbook you will find more pictures of my altar work explaining the work being done on the altar. All you have to do is follow your spirit and your altars will become a powerful space.

I hope you have an idea now how to begin to set up your own altar. Like I said the altar is a very personal set up. You have to set your altar up in a way that fits you and your spirits, not the way someone might think it should be set up. Always do what is right for you.

THE BIBLE IN CONJURE

I know a lot of folks have issues with Christians and the church. The thing is that the church is man-made. Man rules the churches. Most of the folks that go to church worry about what they are going to wear or what Dick and Jane are doing; than what Gods word is saying. I've never had a bad experience with Christians or the church and I'm shocked to hear that so many have, but the thing is humans run these churches and to err is human. The thing is you can't throw the baby out with the bath water if you want to be a Conjurer. The Bible is the meat of Conjure; it is the power behind the work. Some would argue this point and that is their right to do so.

The Bible is a book of power, if you want to learn Traditional Conjure then you must work with the Bible. Actually I was taught to work with the Old Testament and that is what I work with, although there are something's in the New Testament that I have learned to work with. You don't have to be a Christian, you can be anything you want to be but if you are going to claim to be a Conjure worker you need to know how to do the work. Why would you want to waste your time doing some watered down mess when you can do the real deal?

That book we call a Bible is a Tome of power, and when you pray the chapters and verses over your work you are creating a powerful force, one that will get the job done. You don't ever have to set foot in a church if you choose not to, just work with the Bible. God has many names and I personally don't care what name you call him or her as long as you do Conjure the way the work is supposed to be done. If you have to change it to suit you then you need to find something else that works for you! Plain and simple! Prayer builds power and power leads to success! I know some folks don't know how to pray, so if you are one of those folks then just start out by talking. Say what is in your heart, don't worry about if you are doing it right or not. Just DO IT! You have to start somewhere. Conjure is not a religion but it is built around the Bible, the Trinity and prayer.

I can't speak for the folks in Africa because I have never been there although I did have a lady come all the way from Africa to learn from me; she stayed the whole weekend with me. I ask her about this type of work over there and she told me that if you got caught doing this work where she is from you could be stoned by the people and even run out of town. If it is a lie she is the one that told it. One thing I do know is that he Bible is part of Conjure maybe not in what folks are calling New Orleans Hoodoo but it is in Southern Conjure.

I don't dispute the fact that when the ancestors were stolen from Africa they were not Christian. I'm sure they weren't; but I know my history of the South. I was raised on it. This was a whole new world to them. Different language, different food, different clothes, different houses, DIFFERENT ROOTS

AND HERBS, everything in this new world of horror was different. The only thing that couldn't be taken from them was their KNOWLEDGE! It is obvious that they held on to some of their knowledge because we still practice Conjure today; but let's be honest just for a minute. Let's go back in time and take a look at the real horror these great Ancestors who endured a brutality not many could survive.

When they were captured they were chained in the bottom of the ship, they were allowed to wash when the body odor became so bad the sailors couldn't stand the smell any longer. My dogs are kept better than these Ancestors were. Then once they reached the Carolina's that wasn't much better. They were stood up on platforms and inspected the way you would cattle. They checked their teeth, privates and God only knows what else was done to them. Then they were sold. They became the property of another human and "I question that". So woo hoo we be home! If you believe that then you better go read your history books.

They had no homes, they lived in shacks. They were abused and treated less than animals; so do you REALLY believe they were allowed to keep their religion. They would have been looked at as devils or witches; if they would have lived after those Christians "I use the term lightly" got done with them. Unless you have lived in the South you really can't comprehend how it really is. I'm talking about Georgia on up to the Carolina's; even today in 2012 it's a whole different world than the rest of the U.S. I will never believe that they were allowed to have their religious ceremonies amongst their Christian owners. They were smarter than their owners gave them credit and brought Christianity into the work or hid the work inside of Christianity. Conjure is a lot more than what some see as spell work. There are remedies and such that go along with the work; it is a way of life. It is not only about the work. If you try to remove the Bible out of Hoodoo/ Conjure then you are NOT doing Southern Conjure work. You can't separate the two because our Ancestors hid the work in Christianity. I can't speak for New Orleans Voodoo/Hoodoo which folks see as the same thing or that they interchange but I stand firm about Southern Hoodoo/Conjure.

I don't claim to know it all nor do I claim to have a bunch of PHD's next to my name; I have something that money can't buy; the knowledge that has been handed down through my family and my elders. I believe that the Bible is part of the work and always has been. This is what I have seen growing up in a Southern family.

PROPHETS AND SAINTS

MOSES:
THE CONJURE WORKERS PROPHET

"But since then there has not arisen in Israel, a Prophet like Moses, whom the Lord knew face to face, in all the signs and wonders which the Lord sent him to do in the land of Egypt before Pharaoh, before all the servants, and in all his land, and by all that mighty power and all the great terror which Moses performed in the sight of all Israel" (Deuteronomy 34:10-12).

Moses was Gods Favorite Prophet; God favored him the most. Moses wrote the first five books of the Old Testament. He is considered the ancestor of Christianity, Judaism, and Islam; Moses is the only Prophet God spoke directly. Moses is the only

one God ever appeared to; he spoke to the other Prophets in dreams or visions to give them instructions. Moses is the only Prophet to see God. God placed Moses in the cleft of the rock to shield him so he wouldn't be harmed. As God passed by Moses saw his back. He's a true two-headed Conjure worker because God anointed Moses with special powers.

As far as I can tell Moses is the first root doctor in the Bible. In *Leviticus 14 V 1-9* you can see that God gave Moses a recipe to heal the leper. This is where spiritual bathing came from. In *Leviticus 14 V 4-7* Moses tells the priest what to do. Some of this is still practiced today in some religions. There are those who will cleanse a client with a living bird. The bird has to be spiritually dressed before the cleansing and then after the cleansing they set the bird free. I have also seen birds set inside a house or a business, they are brought from room to room soaking up whatever crossed conditions that maybe there. Once it is deemed the place is clean the birds are set free. I think this practice has carried through from Biblical times. Even today cedar wood and hyssop is used in cleansing work. Scarlet which is the deep red like our blood represents the blood of Jesus; or so I was taught.

> *4 then the priest shall command to take for him who is to be cleansed two living and clean birds, cedar wood, scarlet, and hyssop.*
> *5 And the priest shall command that one of the birds be killed in an earthen vessel over running water.*
> *6 As for the living bird, he shall take it, the cedar wood and the scarlet and the hyssop, and dip them and the living bird in the blood of the bird that was killed over the running water.*
> *7 And he shall sprinkle it seven times on him who is to be cleansed from the leprosy, and shall pronounce him clean, and shall let the living bird loose in the open field.*

In Exodus the second book of Moses with God leading him Moses freed his people from Pharaoh; he brought forth ten plagues upon the land of Egypt on God's order. Look at the list of plagues God gave Moses the power to bring forth; they show how powerful Moses really is.

In *Exodus 7:17–18* he turned the water into Blood; the first plague happened when God told Moses to tell Aaron to raise his rod over the Nile and turn the water to blood. *Exodus 8:1–4* there were the frogs; *Exodus 8:16–17* the Gnats; *Exodus 8:20–21* the flies; *Exodus 9:1-3* were hear about all the diseased livestock; *Exodus 9:8-12* God brought boils which is a skin disease; *Exodus 9:13–24* he brought thunder and hail; *Exodus 10-4* Moses brought in the locusts; in *Exodus 10 V21-22* we see that he brought total darkness; finally the last plague in *Exodus 11 V4-5* we see that Moses was order to bring death to every firstborn. Moses was given power that no other human has ever been given.

God even ordered him to punish his own people when they strayed from the path God had laid out for them in order for them to get to the Promised Land. God gave Moses the power to heal the Israelites of poisons, he destroyed their enemies, conquered all blocks that were put in their way, and he also provided everything his people needed to survive. Moses is remembered by Conjure workers, descendants of African slaves, and poor oppressed white folks as a powerful two headed doctor who will work with both hands to set his people free. Ole folks will tell you "Moses didn't go up the mountain; he is the mountain". You can petition Moses through prayer. Go Down Moses is an old spiritual that the slaves prayed to Moses so he could set them free from the white man's chains. Anytime you are feeling down, sing his song and ask Moses to set you free.

As a two headed Conjure doctor Moses can be petitioned for any purpose. He is especially good at cleansing, uncrossing, and reversal work. If you feel like you are being held down you can call on Moses to uncross you with his Conjure stick; don't have a Conjure stick? Let's make one!

1. Find you a tree limb that is about four feet long and big enough around to fit in your hand.
2. Strip all the bark from the limb while praying to Moses.
3. Ask Moses to fill the Conjure Stick with his power.
4. Once you have the limb stripped let it cure (dry out).
5. Every day as the Conjure stick is curing hold the stick in your hands and then you call on Moses ask him to fill the Conjure stick with his power.
6. Make a holy oil out of Olive Oil you have prayed *Psalm 23* into.
7. Once the Conjure stick is cured dress it daily for twenty-one days while calling on Moses to empower it with his power.
8. Once you have it ready you can decorate if you want to.

Work with your Conjure stick when you have a tough job that needs to be done call on Moses by tapping your Conjure stick on the floor three times while calling his name. If you read the five books of Moses you will find different ways to petition Moses.

Here's an example when Moses first petitioned Pharaoh to set his people free he and his brother Aaron threw their Conjure sticks on the ground and they turned into snakes. So Pharaoh summoned his magicians who accomplished the same feat. Moses decided to prove Gods power was stronger than that of the magicians; his and Aarons Conjure sticks ate Pharaoh's snakes.

From my studies of the five books of Moses I believe that he was the strongest and the most favored of all God's Prophets. So in effect the power that Moses has is strongest any human has ever been anointed with by God. He is undefeatable.

If you feel you are crossed up you can petition Moses working with a white vigil and about a foot of thin chain.

1. Cleanse yourself off with the chain and then the white vigil starting at the crown of your head to the bottom of your feet; then break the chain in half

2. Petition Moses to destroy any cross conditions you may have on you; just like he destroyed the snakes Pharaoh's magicians tried to use against him and Aaron
3. Wrap the broken pieces around the white vigil in a circle and light the candle
4. Go to your set up and petition Moses daily to destroy any cross conditions; once the candle goes out throw the pieces of chain in two separate crossroads away from your home

Moses took care of his people; he led them into the Promised Land. Moses protected his people, fed them, clothed them, housed them, he took care of their every need. This tells me that he can be petition for anything we may need in life. Moses works fast when it comes to monies being owed you. Someone owed me $300.00 I petitioned Moses for my money because all I was getting was excuses. This money had nothing to do with spiritual work; within two hours I had my money in my hand. If you are in need of money, food, and shelter ask Moses to bless you.

1. Light a white vigil in a bowl of condensed milk, some honey, and red wine
2. Call on Moses and tell him the offering is for him
3. Ask him for what you need
4. After the vigil burns out pour the mixture outside near your front door

Why milk and honey you may be asking; remember in the Bible it speaks of a place where milk and honey flow along with streets of gold.

Moses parted the Red Sea with his Conjure rod so his people could get across to safety then he let the waters collapse on Pharaoh's men. This shows that Moses can and will do all types of defense work. You can petition Moses for help with cut and clear work, separation work, and any work where you need block or you need to remove somebody or a situation out of your life.

If you want to separate a couple cut the photo of the couple together in half.

1. Place one half going one way and the other half facing down so the couple will be head to toe.
2. Sprinkle a line of sea Salt between the two photos; place three white candles on the line of Salt between them.
3. Light your candles.
4. Then pray your petition to Moses; petition Moses to separate the couple just like he separated the Red Sea.

In *Exodus 11 V 4-7* God proclaimed that not a dog would move his tongue against the children of Israel when Moses went out into the streets to bring death to all the firstborn. To protect your home from being crossed you can make a wash. You need:

> Holy Water from the church
> A pinch of Gunpowder
> A half of cup of red wine vinegar

1. Tear verse 7 out of the Bible, burn it to ash while praying and petitioning Moses for protection.
2. Mix all the ingredients together in a spray bottle.
3. Hold the bottle up to your mouth and pray *Exodus 11 V 4-7* into the bottle
4. Petition Moses to protect your home like he did his people when God inflicted Egypt with the tenth and deadliest plague: death to all firstborn Egyptian males.
5. Spray over all doorways and window sills in your home.
6. Leave a white candle burning by your front door.

> *4 And Moses said, Thus saith the LORD, About midnight will I go out into the midst of Egypt:*
>
> *5 And all the firstborn in the land of Egypt shall die, from the first born of Pharaoh that sitteth upon his throne, even unto the firstborn of the maidservant that is behind the mill; and all the firstborn of beasts.*
>
> *6 And there shall be a great cry throughout all the land of Egypt, such as there was none like it, nor shall be like it any more.*

*7 But against any of the children of Israel shall not
a dog move his tongue, against man or beast: that
ye may know how that the LORD doth put a
difference between the Egyptians and Israel.*

All the Prophets of the Bible are very special in their own way but there is no Prophet like Moses nor can his power be matched. Moses was Gods right hand man. I think God tested him more than he did any other Prophet but Moses never gave up.

THE PROPHET ELIJAH

I had only heard about the Prophet Elijah in church a few
times when the preacher was preaching about Jezebel. I think
most folks know the story of Jezebel. Then one day I was in a
shop looking for a statue, and I see a statue of the Prophet Elijah.
I could not take my eyes off of the statue. I had never seen what
I thought was a Saint holding another person down under their
foot with a sword drawn. If you look at the picture above you
will see what I am talking about. I found the lady that owns the
store and I ask her about the statue; she told me that it was Saint
Elias. She didn't even remember ordering that statue, I thought
that was odd. I ask her more questions about him than she could
answer; so she got her book that tells about all the saints.

She found him under the name Elijah. Elijah was one of
Gods powerful Prophets; he was a man of God like Moses. In
his time the worship of one God became weak among the tribes
of Israel. That is when Jezebel introduced the worship of the god
Baal. Jezebel was the wife of Ahab. Jezebel enlisted a procession
of idol worshipping priests and erected temples to Baal, who was
seen as a god of nature whose powers were greater than God
of Moses. Elijah fought against the evils of the priests of Baal.
He preached about one God with power and passion to those
who had lost faith he brought many back into the fold. A power
struggle went on between him and Queen Jezebel. She hated
this Prophet of God and wanted him dead. She wanted to prove
his God had no power.

It all came to a head when Jezebel challenged him. Jezebel
intensified her efforts to disprove Elijah. She wanted to test the
powers of God and those of Baal; she would later regret this
choice. She decided they would test both God and Baal to see
who had the most power. They set up two altars with sacrifices
on each altar. Each side her priests against God Prophet; the test

was to see who could call down fire to ignite the offerings. The winner would be who ever lit the first fire.

Queen Jezebel herself appeared at the altar; to support her priests. They were given the chance to go first to call down the power to light the fire. They prayed and petitioned Baal, until they finally gave up in disgust. Then the Prophet Elijah came forward; on his first prayer and petition the fire came to life, finally the on-lookers realized the truth at last. They were so furious that they swooped down on the false priests and killed them all. Elijah wasn't done he called for an end to the drought that had parched the land for three years. Upon his prayer and petition the sky opened up and blessed rain fell to feed the once dry earth. Afterwards Elijah went to Mt. Sinai, the same mountain where God had spoken to Moses. Elijah became a powerful Prophet in his own right. As you can see from the picture above he is a tough Prophet who will dole out justice as it is needed. Although I have found he can have a soft touch when petitioned he is the Prophet to call on for hard works as in enemy work.

You can call on the Prophet Elijah for reversal work. You need:

A tin can
A white candle
Some Whiskey

1. Petition Prophet Elijah and ask him to reverse any work or any crossed condition you might have on you.
2. Do this while you are wiping yourself downward with the white candle.
3. Place your candle in a tin can and pour about two inches of Whiskey in the can as an offering.
4. Light your candle.
5. Make your petition daily when the hands of the clock are going downward.

Nail Down an Enemy

There are times when you have to get tough. You have to put your foot down and say enough is enough. This is a harsh work but sometimes it has to be done. For this work you need:

Tea lights, black ones if you can find them
A medicine bottle
A flat head nail
Dirt from a crossroads near your targets home
A photo of the target
Whiskey
A pinch of Sulfur

1. Pray and petition the Prophet Elijah ask him to nail your enemy down so they can't harm you or yours.
2. Hold the photo of your enemy in your hands while you are praying.
3. Fold the photo away from you one fold.
4. Take the nail and run it through the photo.
5. Go through the top of the photo and come out the bottom; making your petition the whole time.
6. Place the photo in the medicine bottle upside down.
7. Add your other ingredients to the bottle; hold the bottle close to your mouth then make your petition.
8. Close the bottle and shake it as hard as you can.
9. Light a tea light and place it on top of the bottle.

Work the bottle daily until you have your results.

Shut Your Mouth

Sometimes folks just don't know when to keep their mouths shut. They want to tend to everyone's business but their own. If you have a busy body you need to shut up you can petition Prophet Elijah. You need:

A flat head nail

A photo of the target

A bottle of Habanera hot sauce

1. Pour a little of the hot sauce so you will have room to add your packet to the bottle.

2. Fold the photo away from you one fold, take the nail and run it through the photo.

3. Go through the top of the photo and come out the bottom; making your petition the whole time.

4. Stick the packet into the bottle of hot sauce.

5. Flip the bottle away from you while you petition Prophet Elijah to shut their mouth and move them out of your way.

6. Get a small glass and turn the bottle upside down in the glass. Look at the photo above.

7. You can burn a tea light on the bottle daily after you work it.

HALT ENEMY CONJURE TRICK

Elijah was stubborn in his faith and faced many trials. If you are being challenged unfairly or put to the test by your enemies you can petition Elijah in this work to bring your enemies to a COMPLETE HALT.

For this work you'll need a firecracker. I use an M-60 explosive for this job because they are loud and you can open the lid. Since the lids can come on and off that means you can load this firecracker with work but you have to be careful because you are dealing with gunpowder and an explosive.

1. Take a photo of your enemy and burn it to ash.
2. Make sure the ash has no cinders or flame.
3. Open the top of the firecracker and load your ash into it.
4. Close the lid.
5. Write your enemy name all over the firecracker.
6. Cross out the name with a black permanent marker until you can't see it.
7. Petition Elijah to protect from your enemy and knock them on their ass.
8. Then take the firecracker to a cross-roads with a STOP sign and ignite the explosive in front of the sign.
9. When you light the explosive don't hold it in your hands.
10. Leave three cents change and walk away.

If you can't use an M-60 explosive then use a regular firecracker. Since they tend to be smaller what you can do is tape the ash from your enemy photo around the fire- cracker.

THE PROPHET ISIAH

The book of Isaiah is a very powerful book in the Bible. This is one of my favorite Prophets. Isaiah is not one to play around, when he is petitioned he is a force to be reckoned with. In *Isaiah 6* you will find a work to cause confusion on a target. God gave the Prophet Isaiah the power to cause confusion. Are you wondering how this all started? Well it all started with a dream Isaiah had about God. In *Isaiah 6 V 1- 6* you will see that Isaiah dreamed he saw God sitting on his throne. There were Seraphs flying over head; each one had six wings. As the Seraphs flew they called to each other *"Holy, holy, holy is the LORD of hosts; the whole earth is full of his glory."* The whole house shook and filled with smoke. In verse 5 the Prophet Isaiah cries out "Woe is me! I am lost, for I am a man of unclean lips, and I live among a people of unclean lips; yet my eyes have seen the King, the LORD of hosts!" Can you imagine how terrified he was even in a dream? One of the Seraphs picked up a hot coal off the altar and flew towards him. In verse 7 it tells us that the Seraphs touched his lips with the hot coal to cleanse them.

God had a mission for Isaiah and from his mission we will get our first work "the work of confusion". Some- times folks just can't or want leave you alone. They are like a dog with a bone. If you find that no matter what you do you can't shake this person then it is time to make "the Confusion Medicine Bottle". This work will confuse your enemy and they won't be able to bother you. In *Isaiah 6 V 9-13* you will see that God gave Isaiah the power to lay people down in a state of confusion.

1. Get a medicine bottle and wash it in vinegar let the bottle air dry.
2. Tear *Isaiah 6 V 9-13* out of the Bible,
3. Write the targets name on the four corners and in the center.

4. Burn the verses to ash; then put them in the bottle.

5. Hold the bottle close to your mouth and petition God and the Prophet Isaiah to confuse the target so they will leave you alone.

6. To the bottle add:

    Black Mustard Seeds,

    Sulfur,

    Gunpowder

    A photo of the target.

7. Set the bottle in a cross set up and burn on it daily.

8. Shake the bottle well while praying your petition.

The Prophet Isaiah also had the sight. He foretold the coming of Jesus and all the suffering he would go through. You can read all about it in *Isaiah 53*. When you need to see what is going on you can call on him to show you in your dreams what you need to know.

1. Light a small white candle;

2. Call on Isaiah petition him to show you what you need to know in your dreams.

3. Place a clear glass of water beside your bed to feed his spirit.

He will bring your answer. He brought me one of my ancestors. I had been petitioning for an ancestor to help me with something, he brought me my great aunt Cora Mabell. She told me her name and I did a search, sure enough she is my great aunt. You can also petition him for protection or you can send him out after an enemy; he's also good to petition when you need a cleansing or road opening work.

If you find yourself in need of a cleansing you can take five bathes with:

    1 cup strong black coffee,

    4 tbls table Salt,

    1 cap of Lemon Juice.

In the old days when I was first taught this bath you used ammonia instead of Lemon Juice.

1. Add all the ingredients into a tub of hot water as the hands of the clock are going downward.
2. Petition the Prophet Isaiah and ask him to remove all blocks and crossed conditions.
3. Then read *Isaiah 41*.

You can do this before, during or after the spiritual bath.

Below you will find two simple prayers that can be prayed on an enemy. Light a candle and petition Isaiah to defeat all your enemies known and unknown.

PRAYERS AGAINST ENEMIES

Isaiah 41:11-12

> Behold, all they that were incensed against thee shall be ashamed and confounded: they shall be as nothing; and they that strive with thee shall perish. Thou shalt seek them, and shalt not find them, even them that contended with thee: they that war against thee shall be as nothing, and as a thing of nought.

Isaiah 54:17

> No weapon that is formed against thee shall prosper; and every tongue that shall rise against thee in judgment thou shalt condemn. This is the heritage of the servants of the Lord, and their righteousness is of me, saith the Lord.

THE PROPHET JOSHUA

Joshua was a major figure in the events of the Exodus, he was Moses apprentice. He was with Moses part of the way to Mount Sinai where Moses received the Ten Commandments. He was one of the twelve spies that Moses sent to explore and report back what they found in the land of Canaan. If you read the book of Joshua you will see that the Prophet Joshua had a hell of a job to do. God sent Joshua to Jericho, where there was a wall built around the city that couldn't be torn down. The Bible tells us that no one came out and no one could go in; that is until God gave Joshua the power to tear down those walls that were unbeatable. There are many powerful works that can be found in the Bible. The tearing down of the walls of Jericho is just one of them. This is practiced in many ole timey churches. This is a very powerful prayer that will tear down the walls that hold you. This work will remove any condition that is holding you down. I first learned this when I was about twelve years old in church. There is nothing that this work can't remove. It may seem like a lot of work but if you have a blocked or crossed condition then it is worth the effort.

The work is started when the hand of the clock is going downward, like at five minutes after the hour. I have done this work a few different ways but I am going to give you an easy way to do it.

1. In the wax of a white glass vigil write your name close to the glass.
2. Around the wick write, "tear down those walls".
3. Call on the Prophet Joshua and say your petition over your candle and then light the candle.
4. Set your candle in the middle of the floor, walk around the candle going counterclockwise (to remove) while you are praying your verses.

Once you have finished snuff your candle out until the next day then repeat the process. On the last day let the candle burn completely out. This prayer is done for seven days, seven times, each day you say the prayer you drop one of the prayers, so you start saying it seven times the first day then the next day it's six times, then five times and so on until the last day you say it only once.

Or you can hold your candle in your hands while you walk counterclockwise praying. If you hold your candle then you only make one pass a day. Leave your candle burning and just pick it up again the next day; do this until you have finished seven days. No matter which way you decide to do the work remember to dress yourself afterward. Prophet Joshua can be petitioned for any kind of work from cleansings to justice work. He is also good to call on when you go against an enemy; he is well versed in war. Since he was a spy for Moses he is good to call upon to see what your enemies are up too. Below you will find two useful works; you never know when you will have need of them. The first one is used to block your enemy and close their roads.

To Block an Enemy

1. Get the dirt from the nearest crossroads to your targets home
2. To this dirt add:
   A photo of the target burned to ash
   Red Pepper
   Sulfur
   Enough vinegar to make a mud patty
3. Roll the patty into a ball, get you two mirrors
4. Place the patty on the side of the mirror you look in; then cover it with the other mirror. So the front and back have the backside of the mirror showing
5. Take some red thread and bound the mirrors into a packet
6. Get a box and paint it black inside and out
7. Once the box is dry put a mixture of the crossroads dirt, Sulfur and Red Pepper in the bottom of the box

8. Set the packet in the box and cover it with the rest of the mixture
9. Burn tea lights in the box daily for twenty-one days while you pray and petition the Prophet Joshua to block your enemy

After the twenty-one days close the box up and put it in a safe place.

LET ME SEE

Sometimes there are things going on that we just can't figure out; something hidden.

1. Get a jar of water and add a little Ms. Stewarts bluing to it
2. Set the jar on a small round mirror
3. Place a photo of the target on the jar looking into the jar
4. And then place a blue candle burning behind the jar
5. Dress your forehead with some Olive Oil that you prayed *Psalm 23* into
6. Then call on the Prophet Joshua
7. Petition him to show you what the target is doing
8. Remind him of the time he spied for Moses
9. Petition him to let you see what your target is hiding

Look deep into the jar of water and you will see what is hidden.

Songs of Solomon

The Prophet Solomon is best known for his wisdom. In *1 Kings* you can read *3 V 11-12* God granted him his petition for wisdom since that is all he asked for. The book called Song of Songs is the book of Solomon it is filled with verses that can be applied to Love Conjure. I think that one of the problems now a day is that folks don't know how to read the Bible. They just don't have an understanding of the power this book holds. I'm not preaching; I'm trying to make folks understand that they have the means to be successful in all their works if they would just get a Bible and put the words to use. Don't misunderstand me; I'm not talking about church or being a Christian. What I am saying is take the Bible and read it like you would any other book.

There are eight chapters in the Song of Solomon; each book has about 14 to 17 verses in it. This is one of the most read books in the Bible and the least understood. Folks get confused because of the wording; but you don't have to apply a whole thing to your love work. You can pick the verses that you are drawn to. You would work with these verses just like you do the psalm in your work. The trick here is to find a verse or verses that deal with the love work you are doing. I am going to give a few examples and try to explain how they would be applied to love work or come to me work. These are just examples; I'll first show you how easy it can be to add the Bible to your Conjure work. Then we will move on to the work.

The first chapter and verse I picked. chapter 2 v 14.

> *O my dove, that art in the clefts of the rock,*
> *in the secret places of the stairs, let me see thy*
> *countenance,*

This could be used in Conjure work to bring someone to you, if you did the work as a compelling and a come to me work.

> *let me hear thy voice;*

You can work with this to make someone call you, not only to call you but to be sweet to you when they call.

for sweet is thy voice, and thy countenance is comely.

The next one is *Chapter 2 v 16;* I picked this one because you are making a statement here. He belongs to you and you belong to him; this could be used to tie someone to you.

My beloved is mine, and I am his: he feedeth among the lilies.

I would combine both of these verses together to draw someone too me and to nail them down so they would stay. There are so many chapters and verses in the Bible that can help us; in all of your Conjure work if we just look for them.

COME TO ME MEDICINE BOTTLE

You need:

A medicine bottle of any kind
A magnet
Something of the targets
Lovage
Master of the Woods
A square headed nail
Dixie John
Some Aunt Jemima syrup

1. Lay all your ingredients out on a white handkerchief,
2. Make a cross set up
3. Set a tea light in the center of your ingredients.
4. Call on the Prophet Solomon; petition him to draw your target to you.
5. Pray your petition and 2 V 16 over the ingredients.
6. Place all the ingredients in the medicine bottle;
7. Hold the bottle up to your mouth call on Solomon to fill the bottle full of his power.

8. Pour enough syrup into the medicine bottle to cover your ingredients.
9. Pray into the bottle one more time the close the lid.
10. Shake the bottle while praying your petition.

I'm going to give each Chapter, the verses for the work and a small work that can be done. I was going to write this section a little different but I think it's best to get to the meat of the work.

Chapter 1 V2-4 Drawing Conjure

If you look at the verses below you will see that they are drawing the target to them. You need:

A photo of the target
Sugar
Two magnets
A bowl
Red wine
A red candle

1. Write your petition across the face of the target.
2. Place the picture between two magnets.
3. Make a bed of Sugar in the bottom of the bowl.
4. Place the photo on the bed then cover it with Sugar.
5. Hold the candle up to your mouth and petition Solomon and ask him to draw your target to you.
6. Set the candle in the bowl and light it.
7. Repeat your petition and pour the red wine into the bowl.

Go everyday as the hands of the clock are moving upward and pray your petition over your work.

2 Let him kiss me with the kisses of his mouth!
For your love is better than wine,

3 your anointing oils are fragrant,
your name is perfume poured out;
therefore the maidens love you.

4 Draw me after you, let us make haste.
The king has brought me into his chambers.
We will exult and rejoice in you;
we will extol your love more than wine;
rightly do they love you.

CHAPTER 2 V8—10 COME TO ME WORK

Sometimes the simplest works are the strongest. For this work you need:

1. Two candles one to represent yourself the other one becomes your target
2. Place your photo looking outward on your candle
3. Glue a magnet over the heart area
4. Take *2 V 8-10* and burn them to ash
5. Place your dressed candle and the ash in a bowl
6. light your candle while saying your prayer
7. Fill the bowl with syrup
8. Put your targets photo on their candle
9. Glue a magnet over their heart area
10. Dress their candle, say your prayers and light their candle
11. Set their candle away from yours and move it slowly daily while saying your petition for them to come to you

8 The voice of my beloved!
Look, he comes, leaping upon the mountains,
bounding over the hills.
9 My beloved is like a gazelle or a young stag.
Look, there he stands behind our wall, gazing in
at the windows, looking through the lattice.
10 My beloved speaks and says to me:
'Arise, my love, my fair one, and come away;

CHAPTER 3 I SEE YOU

In verse 2 it says:

"I will seek him whom my soul loves"

Then it goes on to say that she found him. You can petition Solomon to help you find you lost love.

1. Take *3 V 1- 4* out of the Bible and burn it to ash.
2. Sprinkle the ash in a bowl of clear water.
4. Light a white candle and place it behind the bowl.
5. Petition Solomon to help you find your target and to let you see what they are doing.

CHAPTER 6 V2-3 KEEP EM FAITHFUL

For this work you need:

> A square of Red Flannel
> Some cotton string
> A pinch of Lovage
> Master of the Woods
> And Calamus
> A photo of you and your target
> And a square head nail

1. Lay out your flannel
2. Fold your photo where you and your target are facing each other
3. Run the nail through the photo's
4. Hold the photo up to your mouth call on the Prophet Solomon
5. Then pray your petition
6. And then lay the photo on your flannel
7. Cover your photo with the herbs and fold the flannel into a packet.
8. Wrap the packet while you are praying
9. Once the packet is tied up feed it a little Whiskey
10. Repeat your prayer and petition to Solomon

Place your packet between your mattresses on the targets side of the bed.

CHAPTER 8 BRING EM HOME

There are times when we are separated from our love ones by choice or something else. This is a work that can be done when it seems like they don't want to come home.

1. Make a Dollie either out of Red Flannel or a piece of clothing that belong to the target
2. Stuff the Dollie with cotton because cotton absorbs
3. Load the Dollies head with whatever roots and herbs you want too
4. Place the face of the target on the Dollies face
5. Name the Dollie for the target
6. Petition Solomon and pray 8 V 3-4 and 5-7 V 14
7. Get a fishing hook and some fishing line. Hook the Dollie in the head; make sure you call on your target
8. And pray to Solomon to bring them home
9. Go out the back door and come in the front door while you "reel" your target back in the house
10. Do this daily until you get your result

There are many different ways you could work the verses in the book of Solomon. I just shared a few works. The same verses can be used in all love works you do. The best way to understand the verses is to read your Bible. There are tons of works in the Bible if you just look with your eyes wide opened.

MOTHER MARY

There is almost nothing written about petitioning Mother Mary in Hoodoo/Conjure. That's because folks don't know how if they did it would be written about in books or it would be plastered all over the internet. As a child I was taught how important Mary was because she was Jesus's mama. Mary is all about the family especially the sons, but like St. Martha she too can have a strong firm hand.

Any Mother that is worth a grain of Salt is going to protect her children. Mother Mary is very good when it comes to protection. You can petition her for protection in any situation you may find yourself in. I have found that when working with her she likes plain ole Olive Oil when you are dressing her vigils and work. From experience it seems to me that she works faster if the petition is for a male child; a son or Grandson. I burn white candles for her. She doesn't need a bunch of Hocus Pocus to get her to help you; just petition her.

She can also be petitioned for healing. If you find yourself in need of some healing work then; take a white un- dressed candle. Call on the Trinity then on Mother Mary. Petition her to aid in the healing of your body. She works really fast when it comes to opened wounds and pain.

1. Take the candle and rub it over the affected area
2. The pain will ease in no time
3. Let the candle burn out and repeat as needed

She really helps with a woman's monthly suffering.

I want to share one small work that can be done with her; I would share more but I don't want my work changed around a little and claimed by others as their own.

PROTECTION MEDICINE BOTTLE

Isaiah 43 torn from the Bible and burned to ash
A photo of the family burned to ash
Frankincense
Devils Bit
Devils Shoestring
A Pinch of dirt from a church yard
Pour in some Olive Oil

1. While you are making the bottle pray and petition Mother Mary for protection.
2. Once you have the bottle ready, set it on top of a photo of the Holy Family in front of a statue of the Mother Mary.
3. Set four tea lights around the bottle in the sign of the cross.
4. Light them and pray your petition.

Once the bottle is finished give it to her for safe keeping go at least once a week and renew your petition.

SAINT PETER

*S*aint Peter holds the keys to heaven; he is the keeper of all the gates, doors and roads. You can call upon him for all types of work but I think he is best known for his road opening work. A lot of folks are afraid of St. Peter and won't work with him. They say he is a dangerous dark Saint. I think it is because he was crucified on the cross upside down, and that is why so many fear him. He did this because he didn't think he was as good as Jesus to be crucified upright. There was no deep dark reason; he did it out of respect. I have found nothing about him working with him all these years that would make me fear him. He is a saint that will do either light or dark work depending on the work being done. He can close your roads just as easy as he can open them.

His symbol is two small gold keys crossed over each other held together with red thread. You can burn a red, blue, orange or you can burn a road opening candle when calling on Saint Peter to come to your aid. To petition Saint Peter tap on the floor three times using your Conjure stick while you call his name. You call his name on each tap. Then you can say something like

"St. Peter open the roads,
open the roads so _____ can come in.
Open the roads Saint Peter
Open the roads."

As an offering you can give Saint Peter either Whiskey or red wine he likes either one. I have found he also likes iron; I added some to his bottle of Whiskey he seems to like it. If you need to open your roads:

1. Collect the dirt from the four corners of the crossroad nearest your house
2. Place a large magnet and the dirt it in a bowl
3. Then get the dirt from your front door, add this to the bowl

4. Cover the dirt and magnet with change out of your wallet
5. Then cover all of it with Sugar
6. Take a candle and dress it
7. Then petition Saint Peter to open your roads
8. Place the candle in the bowl and light it
9. Pour some red wine into the bowl as an offering

Place your bowl behind your front door and go daily to pray and petition Saint Peter.

St Peter — Money Packet Prosperity Cleanse

Sometimes you might find yourself in a tight financial bind. We all go through financial hardships. No one is the exception including Conjure workers. In all my 40+ years of being an old school worker I wouldn't know anything about prosperity work nor would I be good at drawing money if it wasn't for all the trials and financial hardships I faced. I've taken care of people my whole life including my kids, grandkids, cousins, siblings, and loved ones. People have always turned to me for help whether for Conjure work or because financially they are in a huge bind and need some help. I had to learn at an early age how to face poverty otherwise that means no food on the table for me and my family. I refuse to this day to let that happen! As long as God allows me to stay alive I will never let my children nor my loved ones starve nor go without!!! That is the mentality you need to have if you want to be successful in money drawing and prosperity work.

No one likes to struggle for money but I believe that sometimes these trials really what we say they are: "trials!" They are a test from God to see how strong we are. It's only when we're struggling with an ongoing issue that we find our inner strength and somehow manage to pull through those hardships. Look at the lives of all the Prophets and saints old school Conjurers work within Conjure. The Prophets had very hard lives and made great sacrifices that most of the time cost their lives but through those sacrifices they found a power that God instilled in them that brought them to the top of the mountain.

Regardless of the ups and downs in life sometimes everyone needs a little break including me. This work with Saint Peter will do just that. It will ease up financial troubles and change your luck around so your needs will always be met. The hardest lesson to learn in drawing prosperity is to always be grateful for your blessings. When you learn to show gratitude for what you do have instead of focusing on what you don't have God will always bless you with more. Always remember "like begets like."

For this work you will need:

Two skeleton keys
Green ribbon
Red string
$5 bill
Two strong magnets
Blue Flag Root
A few grains of rice
Hair from the crown of your head
A pinch of Solomon's Seal Root
Sassafras Root

I prefer to use copper or brass skeleton keys because cop per holds power and brass symbolizes prosperity. You can find these at the antique store but iron keys are okay too for this work. Always remember use what you have and don't limit yourself by what you don't have. That is what Conjure work is all about.

You will also need:

An orange candle,
A white cloth,
A glass of Sugar water with a penny face up inside
  the water.

The Sugar water and orange candle are offerings to Saint Peter. You need the white cloth because you will make a basic altar setup by the front door where luck comes and goes.

1. You need to set up a small altar behind your front door but before you do you need to clean you area
2. Inside a large bowl of water make a wash of
   1 teaspoon Ammonia
   A bit of Sugar
   Salt
   Holy Water
   A pinch of Cayenne Pepper

3. Wipe your space down with this mixture while saying *Psalm 23* and a petition to Saint Peter to open your roads
4. Let the altar and space area dry
5. Drape your altar cloth over your space and burn a little Frankincense and Myrrh

Now your space is ready.

6. Take a pair of skeleton keys and cross them together with both sides facing UP in the SAME DIRECTION.
7. Wrap green ribbon around the crossed keys TOWARDS you while asking Saint Peter to draw money and prosperity to you and all your loved ones.
8. Keep wrapping the green ribbon around the crossed keys until they are secure then tie five knots.
9. State your petition for money drawing as you secure each knot.
10. Place your crossed keys under running water for a few seconds.

The running water will rid the keys of any negativity that may have attached itself.

11. Hold the keys to your mouth close to your breath
12. Say Psalms 23 with a petition for your roads to always be open and prosperous
13. Call on Saint Peter and ask him to fill his keys with power
14. Tell him that you have prepared his keys so he can open your doors for prosperity and total success

I also like to say David's Victory Song (Psalm 20) over the keys because this psalm is powerful. It affirms total success and victory. I'm not a big fan of Psalms but I have to include it because it really does bring success.

15. Dress your crossed keys with holy oil
16. Pass them through the smoke of Frankincense & Myrrh

Your keys are ready to work. Now you need to do a cleansing. For the cleansing part of this work you will wipe yourself down from the crown of your head to the soles of your feet with the orange candle while asking Saint Peter to change your luck for the better and give your life the turn around so you can be a total success.

17. Start from the crown of your head and wipe yourself downward with a orange candle wiping downward to your toes
18. Make sure you clean the back of your neck

Remember you are moving from HEAD to TOE. You may feel a pull from the candle. That candle is pulling blocks on you into the wax which will burn when you light it to Saint Peter.

You can clean yourself as many times that you feel necessary but at least wipe yourself three times from HEAD to TOE. Three is the number of the Trinity.

Now you're going to make a small money packet to draw prosperity in the house. In this work we'll use a $5 bill since five is Saint Peter's number. It represents the four corners of the crossroads with you in the center. You can always use other bills but I prefer number five.

19. Write your full name and your birthday just below the face of the $5 bill with a red pen. Red is hot and brings fast luck.
20. Then write "TOTAL SUCCESS" over your name and cover it with the success symbol ($$¢¢$$).
21. Turn the $5 bill face down.
22. Put some hair from the crown of your head in the center with:
    Blue Flag Root
    Solomon's Seal Root
    Sassafras
    Some grains of rice

You only need a little here and there because a little always goes a long way in Conjure work just like when you're cooking.

24. Fold the bill TOWARDS you covering the ingredients in half
25. Turn the bill CLOCKWISE and fold it towards you again

Repeat this step until you can't fold the $5 bill anymore. By now you got a packet. Make sure you fold it tight so the ingredients won't get loose.

26. Dress only one of the magnets with a drop of Holy oil
27. Then place your money packet between the magnets

You're feeding only one magnet with holy oil because that magnet will draw money to you. The other magnet that isn't dressed will pull blocks from your money. Each time it removes a block the magnet will be fed just like a cleansing candle. If you're creative like me you can paint your magnets in colors that symbolize POWER, TOTAL SUCCESS, & PROSPERITY before you use them. I like purple, gold, red, and green. These are good colors for money work.

28. Now get the Red Cotton String and wrap it around your money packet
29. Always remember to wrap the string towards you turn the packet clockwise
30. Then wrap towards you again until your packet is secure. You wrap the string just like the way you fold the bill towards you when preparing a packet
31. Tie five knots in your packet

Do not cut the string. Make sure you have extra string left to secure your packet to the crossed keys.

32. Wrap your money packet around the crossed keys
33. Using the leftover red string and secure the packet.

Now your money packet is directly tied into success work with Saint Peter. As long as those keys always point up Saint Peter will keep your roads open since all your doors are open.

34. Place the orange candle on the altar

35. Set your crossed keys on the altar pointing UP against the candle

The keys should be leaning on the candle. Remember to make those keys face UP to keep your roads open otherwise you can cross yourself up. We don't want that to happen!

36. Place your Sugar water containing FACE UP penny on the altar to the right of the orange candle
37. Set a bell next to the orange candle on the left

This setup is a straight line with the candle/crossed keys in the middle, the bell to the left, and the Sugar water to the right.

38. Knock three times on the altar
39. Ring the bell three times
40. Light the orange cleansing candle
41. Call Saint Peter to you
42. Tell him the Sugar water, crossed keys holding your packet, and bell is an offering to him so he will open your roads
43. Ask Peter to remove all obstacles to your success and bring you victory

Let the candle burn down. Once a week cleanse yourself with an orange candle and offer a glass of Sugar water. Include a penny in the glass FACE UP. Dispose the old water with penny at a crossroads. This is your payment to Saint Peter for blessing you with prosperity. This work is very simple to keep up and only needs to be repeated once a week if you want to keep the luck coming. I prefer Mondays since Mondays are the first workday of the week. Since you're working then that means you're making money. This work seems like a lot at first because there are so many steps but it's really easy once you get the hang of it. My goal as a teacher, author, spiritual worker, and Conjure woman is to see all of you prosper with TOTAL SUCCESS. That is why I wrote this book because it makes me feel good when I see my students, clients, and readers work to achieve their total BEST. We practice Conjure so we can be blessed for total success.

Reversal Conjure with Iron Keys

St Peter is the door opener, he holds the keys to heaven. He can open or shut the door. I was always taught to petition God and St Peter first before doing any spiritual work. You petition God first because the work belongs to him. Saint Peter removes obstacles. His symbol is a pair of crossed keys.

In this work you will do a cleansing with skeleton keys and reverse any blocks you are facing.

1. First put two skeleton keys under running water
2. Then make the keys into a cross with both keys pointing up
3. Wrap your red string around the skeleton keys AWAY from you
4. While petitioning Saint Peter to remove all blocks from you
5. Hold the crossed keys to your mouth and call the spirit of Peter into those keys
6. Tell the saint the keys you have prepared are his offering to use in cleansing you and removing whatever blocks stand in the way of your prosperity

You will know St Peter is there because you'll feel his spirit.

7. Dress the crossed keys with holy oil
8. Pass them over Frankincense and Myrrh
9. When you pass the keys over the incense make the sign of the cross from top to bottom then right to left. That's North, South, East, and West. The cross opens your roads

You need to do a spiritual cleansing on yourself with Saint Peter's keys and a black/white Reversal candle. If you don't have a Reversal candle, then use a black or a white candle. What's important is that when you cleanse yourself with the crossed keys remember they must point UP. NEVER CLEANSE YOURSELF WITH A PAIR OF CROSSED KEYS POINTING DOWN OR YOU WILL CROSS YOUR ASS UP!!! I'm very serious about this. When you draw something or want to open roads with St Peter you must always work his keys while they're pointing up towards the sky. To do the opposite work or what some folks call "work with the left hand" you want with Saint Peter's keys pointing downward.

10. So take the keys pointing UP and starting at the crown of your head make the sign of the cross over your head.

11. Then proceed downward from your head all the way to your feet making the sign of the cross over your body as you cleanse yourself.

When you make the sign of the cross in Conjure you always do it top to bottom, right to left which is North, South, East, and West. Don't do it like the Catholics from top to bottom and left to right. You don't want to cross yourself up.

12. While you are making those crosses over yourself with the keys pointing UP petition Saint Peter to open your roads and destroy all your enemies known and unknown. Ask God and Peter to turn all your obstacles into opportunities and destroy anybody standing in the way of your blessings.

You'll repeat the same step with your black/white Reversal candle.

13. Starting at the crown of your head cleanse yourself with the Reversal candle by making crosses from top to bottom and right to left

14. Cleanse yourself as you make those crosses from your head to your toe

Don't forget to cleanse those feet.

15. Lay out a square of Red Flannel

16. Place your Reversal candle in the middle of the flannel square.

17. Stand the crossed keys on the Reversal candle pointing up

18. Hold your hands over your work and ask God to trap all your enemies and destroy any work that has been placed on you

19. Light the Reversal candle and say a prayer to St. Peter

For the next four days state your petition over your work for a total of five days.

20. On the fifth day tear out *Deuteronomy 33 V 27-29*
21. Write ALL MY ENEMIES KNOWN & UNKNOWN on the Bible verse and wrap it around the crossed keys pointing down

Deuteronomy 33:27-29

27 The eternal God is thy refuge, and underneath are the everlasting arms: and he shall thrust out the enemy from before thee; and shall say, Destroy them.

28 Israel then shall dwell in safety alone: the fountain of Jacob shall be upon a land of corn and wine; also his heavens shall drop down dew.

29 Happy art thou, O Israel: who is like unto thee, O people saved by the LORD, the shield of thy help, and who is the sword of thy Excellency! And thine enemies shall be found liars unto thee; and thou shalt tread upon their high places.

For the final part of the work you will make a Conjure packet so that your roads will always remain open. This works two ways: (1) it will keep your roads open and (2) it will cross up anybody trying to jinx your blessings.

22. Place the crossed keys in the middle of the red square flannel pointing down
23. Add:
    Five Finger Grass
    Sulfur
    Devil's Bit Root
    Four shiny pennies preferably the ones with the shields to the packet

Use whatever change you have but the new pennies with the shields are best for this work because they symbolize protection.

24. Fold the square flannel AWAY from you until you can't fold it anymore
25. Then wrap red string around the packet away from you in the shape of a cross

Just keep turning the packet and folding your string going away from you until the packet is tied down.

26. Make five knots in your string
27. State your petition as you tie each knot
28. Feed your packet a little Whiskey and holy oil
29. Go to a crossroads where a STOP sign is located and bury your packet in front of the sign
30. Ask Saint Peter to bring all your enemies to a speedy halt and lock them down so they can't bring you anymore trouble

The reason you want to go where two roads cross at the stop sign is because you are bringing all your troubles to a complete HALT.

Your work is finished. Normally you'd pay at the crossroads with a few coins but you already made your payment to Spirit when you included change in the Conjure packet. When the spirits pick up their change at the crossroads they will take the work with them too.

Saint Martha

I have worked with St. Martha for many years; she is all about the hearth and home. She will make sure the woman is in charge if the home, she will make sure your home runs smooth. Saint Martha is not a money saint but you can ask her to help pay the bills and also to keep food on the table. I was taught to never to go her for money per se, only when the money was needed for bills and such. Over the years I have done a lot of work with St. Martha, not only for myself but for clients. St Martha is not real crazy about men. She works hard and fast on them. I know some men claim to work with her; I have never heard of her really helping them. The type of work Saint Martha is known for is not suited for everyone; some workers won't touch it. As I tell all of my students you must always do what is right for you! If you feel a job is wrong then please don't do the work.

St. Martha's day is Tuesday. Green and purple are her main candle colors although I have burn white candles when that was all I had. If you have a job for her you start the work on Tuesday; if that candle burns out before Tuesday wait until Tuesday to light another one. Light another candle on the following Tuesday repeating the same request. I have found that she can be slow in help- ing you. It takes about 2 weeks before you see a big change; but once she gets a hold of them you will start seeing big changes. You have to be consistent when working with her and light a candle every week on Tues- day. I give her an offering of coffee or Whiskey; I always give her the offering before she does the work. I have found for myself I get better results by doing it this way. You can work with her however you please; but I have found she likes her offerings first.

I always ask her to dominate and control them as she does the dragon at her feet. If there is a lot of fussing and angry words being spoken I ask her to silence them. She is a saint for women

and she will deal with men with a heavy hand, although she will work with some men. If you need her and call on her she will be there for you. Not all men are bad but some of them can be really cruel. Saint Martha will set them down.

Bring Him Back

Some men are dogs plain and simple! I am not bashing all men, some of them are very good but then you have those who aren't worth a grain of Salt. There are times when a man must be made to face his commitments and his responsibilities. Some men often think the grass is greener on the other side of the fence. The woman is the one stuck paying the bills and taking care of the children.

If you find yourself in this type of situation then the work below will help you get him back home where he belongs.

Things you need

4 Green Tea Lights
1 Purple candle
Petition
St. Martha prayer card or statue
Photo of the person (if you have one)

Get yourself ready to do the job, and then set up your work space.

1. Place the photo of the target in a tin can
2. Then place your petition on top of the photo
3. Using a nail, write in the wax of the purple candle near the wick:
   "the Lord is my Sheppard I shall not want".
4. Place the candle in the tin can on top of the photo and petition
5. Pour about a half a cup of grape wine into the tin can
6. Take one of each of the tea lights out of their tin and write the person's name on the candle
7. Then dress each of the tea lights with a little oil
8. Place the tea lights back in their tin holders
9. Place the tea lights around the can in the crossroads set up

10. Then you light your candles and call on St. Martha

This is my call to her; you won't find it in any books or on-line.

11. Tap 3 times on the floor with your Conjure Stick in front of her altar then say:

"Holy Mother Martha, I call on you in my time of need I beseech you Mother to hear my call"

12. State your petition then say

"Blessed Mother you have never let me down
Please dominate like you did the dragon under your feet
I ask you Mother to bring him back
Mother make him meek and mild as you did the dragon
Draw him back immediately Mother, don't make me wait another day!
In the name of God the Father,
God the Son,
God the Holy Spirit
and St. Martha
Amen."

SEPARATION PACKET

Saint Martha the Dominator is not only a dominator of men but of all situations where you need to get the upper hand. Sometimes we all need a little push in the right direction or a helping hand when you have jealous coworkers playing kiss ass with the boss, someone competing unfairly against your business, or a scandalous love rival trying to steal your man out of your arms.

For this packet you'll need:

A picture of your man
A picture of the love rival
Snake shed
A square of Red Flannel
Red Cotton String

Lightning struck wood

Grains of Paradise

Master of the Woods

Dirt Daubers Nest

Calamus Root

Alum

Cayenne Pepper

This work is done in a two layer packet then you will work it in an empty baby food jar.

1. The faces of the photos should be facing the opposite so they can't look at each other and head to foot so they'll never talk to each other

2. Light a green vigil candle to Saint Martha and petition her to give you the upper hand

3. Ask her to separate your man and the love rival so you can rule his roost. Tell Saint Martha you are giving her the green vigil to work with so you will be victorious

4. Wrap the snake shed completely around the photos while telling your man to leave the jezebel alone

5. Since you are doing separation work wrap the snake shed AWAY from you

Keep wrapping the photos with the snake shed until they are completely covered.

6. Tie five knots in the snake shed to secure the packet.

7. Lay out the square of Red Flannel on the altar.

8. Place the snake shed packet in the middle of the flannel square. Sprinkle Alum, lightning struck wood, Master of the Woods, Calamus Root, Dirt Daubers Nest, a good amount of cayenne pepper, and Grains of Paradise on the snake sheds.

9. Take the flannel square and fold AWAY from you in half covering the ingredients.

10. Turn the packet counterclockwise and fold AWAY from you in half

Repeat this step until you can't fold the packet anymore.

11. Now you will secure the packet with the red cotton thread

When you tie a packet with red thread you are locking down your work so it can't get out.

12. Wrap the red thread around the packet going AWAY from you turn it counterclockwise and wrap around the packet AWAY from you again
13. When you are done tie nine knots
14. Place the separation packet in a baby food jar
15. Add water from a thunderstorm inside the jar

You can also use stagnant water to bring the relationship to a halt.

16. Close the jar up and shake it
17. State your petition in a loud firm voice
18. Light a red tealight on top of the jar
19. Shake the separation jar and burn a red tealight on top of the jar for a total of nine days

The reason you're using a red tealight because red brings heat and confusion while the metal tin from the tealight will heat up your work as it gets hot. Once a week burn a tealight on top of your jar. Keep working it until you see results.

St. Martha's Prayer

"St. Martha, I resort to thy aid and protection. As proof of my affection and faith, I offer thee this light, which I shall burn every Tuesday. Comfort me in all my difficulties and through great favors thou didst enjoy when the Savior was lodged in thy house, intercede for my family."

SAINT MICHAEL

St. Michael is the prince of the Heavenly host. In other words he is the angel closest to God because he is the prince of Heaven. St. Michael is God's hit man who will bring vengeance and justice on the wicked. His name Michael means *"Who is Like God"* so now you see how strong he really is! His colors are red and white and his feast day is September 29th. St. Michael is not only a protector of the innocent but a defender of righteousness and truth. Call on St. Michael to hold your enemies down like he did the demon under his feet; you can petition St. Michael and ask him to put the fiery wall of protection around you when you are in grave danger or need protection. St Michael's symbol is the sword of justice. This sword can be used either for protection or to nail your enemies down. For protection St. Michael's sword is placed upwards.

If you have need of St. Michael's great power to nail an enemy down then you take a photo of that enemy or petition paper and place St. Michael's sword going downward on the petition. Ask St. Michael to hold your enemy down like he did the demon under his feet and don't release the enemy until the threat is over.

This work can be used to petition St. Michael to tie and bind your enemy. You need:

> A white handkerchief
> A photo of the person or their name
> And any personal items you have of the person
> Some Red Pepper

1. Place the items in the center of the handkerchief. Fold the handkerchief away from you until it looks like a long rope. Pick up the handkerchief on each end
2. Hold the packet in front of St. Michael and call on St. Michael to bind and block your enemies

3. As you are stating your petition pull the knot as hard as you can pull it and make in a strong firm voice your petition that so and so is bound by the power of St. Michael.

4. Wrap the packet around a red vigil and light it while petitioning St. Michael to bind your enemies.

5. When the vigil has burned out place that packet around the base of St. Michael's statue, while petitioning him to keep the knot strong so that the enemy will not escape like he held the devil under his feet.

If you have an enemy who's causing you trouble and you want to bottle them up and stomp them from harassing and causing you problems place them inside a St. Michael medicine bottle.

1. Write your enemies names on a piece of paper

2. Draw a circle around the names nail your enemies down

3. Then make a cross on the names to lock them

4. Wrap the petition around 3 Devil's Shoestrings

5. and make a packet with Red Flannel

6. Bind up the packet with Red Cotton String

7. and call on St. Michael to tie your enemies under your feet like he did the demon

8. Put the packet in your medicine bottle with
   Some Frankincense
   Sulfur
   Fire ants
   Dirt Daubers Nest,
   Gunpowder.
   Pour Whiskey into the bottle
   Add lots of Red Pepper.

9. Close the bottle up and say in strong voice
   "All my enemies are locked, tied, and bound under my feet. In the name of Jesus I call on

you St. Michael to deliver swift justice to all my
aggressors. Amen"

10. Shake the bottle daily while praying to St. Michael to come to your aid.
11. When you are ready turn the medicine bottle upside down and place on a round mirror with a red tealight at each of the 4 corners and a red tealight in the center on top of the medicine bottle.

Do this work for 9 days or until the threat is over. Put the medicine bottle in a cool dark place or leave it with St. Michael.

St Michael Healing

Most folks don't realize that St. Michael is a great healer. Most folks see St Michael only as a protector and a defender. Since St. Michael is a healer you can call on him to cut through illness and remove all crossed conditions.

1. Take a brown egg and draw a circle on the egg.
2. Make the sign of the cross inside the circle and write the illness on the cross.
3. Take that egg and clean yourself from the top of your head to the bottom of your feet. Don't forget to clean your feet from heel to toe.
4. Petition St. Michael to lock down the illness in the egg and clean you.
5. Once you feel the egg get heavy clean yourself from the top of your head to the bottom of your feet with each red vigil. Don't forget to clean your feet with the vigils from heel to toe.
6. Place the vigils in an upright triangle with the egg in the middle.

Don't feed the vigils with any Conjure Oils or herbs because they will pull the illness off you. The illness is what will feed the vigil lights.

To Bring Back A Lover

This is a work that I have used to help other's bring back a spouse or lover that has left them. This work's really well if you put your all into it. You will need:

A small glass
Spring water
Loveage root
Rose Petals
A magnet
A red heart
A plate
Some honey
A Saint Michael Candle
A red candle
A Black candle
Paper
Pen to write out the petition
A photo of the one you want to come back

Here are the instructions for each of the steps taken. I want to say this if you want something bad enough you have to work for it. You CAN'T just throw everything together and expect it to do all the work for you. You need to pray and put your energies into it. With that said here is how it works. I suggest you set up a nice love altar.

Put photo's of yourself and your loved one in happier times on it
Sprinkle some rose petals on it
Put things that mean love to you on it

This will help you focus and also lend energy to the work.

1. Take the glass and add the spring water, Loveage Root, Rose Petals, and the red heart.
2. Hold both palms over the glass pray to your higher power to give this glass power to do the work you need done.

3. Now place the picture of your loved one upside down in the glass with the face facing out.
4. Set the glass on the plate, make a circle of honey and Loveage around the glass.
5. Now take the red candle and dress it with oil and the name of the person you want to bring back with your name on top of theirs.
6. You can write this out 3, 6 or 9 times.
7. Set this candle behind the plate.
8. To the left of this candle you will place the black candle.
9. Then to the right of the candle you will place the St. Michael candle.
10. Say the St. Michael novena and ask St. Michael to defend this work and for his protection.
11. Now this is important, you have the black candle, red, then your saint candle. Light the red candle first praying over it in your usual way, then the saint candle per instruction and last the black candle.
12. EVERYDAY you will MOVE the black candle away from the other two, a little each day. This will remove all negative energies and past hurts from the situation. If this is done right the loved one should be home soon.

FIERY SWORD PROTECTION PACKET

For this packet you will need:
> A square of Red Flannel
> St Michael sword pendant
> Red Cotton String
> Devil's Shoestring
> Lightning struck wood
> Master of the Woods
> Sage for wisdom
> *Daniel 12 V 1* torn from the Bible

1. Lay your square of flannel on the altar.

Daniel 12 V 1

> *"And at that time shall Michael stand up, the great prince which standeth for the children of thy people: and there shall be a time of trouble, such as never was since there was a nation even to that same time: and at that time thy people shall be delivered, every one that shall be found written in the book."*

2. Write your full name and "ALL MY LOVED ONES" on the Bible verse
3. State your petition
4. Draw a cross on the names and a circle to contain your petition
5. Then place the Bible verse, Devil's Shoestring, lightning struck wood, Master of the Woods, and Sage in the middle of the flannel square
6. Place your hands over the ingredients and ask St Michael to fill your work with power. Say his revocation and call on God to place a fiery wall of protection around you that can't be breached
7. Pour a little Whiskey on the ingredients to feed your work
8. Then hold the square of flannel close to your mouth and state your petition three times over the ingredients where your breath can touch them. I always do this in the name of the Father, Son, & Holy Ghost
9. Place the flannel square back on the altar
10. Fold the square towards you in half covering the ingredients
11. Turn the flannel clockwise and fold it again covering your items.

Basically you are folding the packet in halves until you can't fold it anymore. When you make a protection packet always fold TOWARDS you since you are drawing protection to you and your loved ones.

12. Now you need to secure your packet with the red string. Wrap the string around your packet towards you, turn the packet clockwise, wrap towards you again.

Keep repeating until your packet is tied.

13. Make nine knots.
14. Do not cut the string. Use whatever leftover string you have left to tie the St Michael sword pendant around your packet. When you tie that sword ask Saint Michael to cut down your enemies and hold them under your feet just like he held the devil under his feet.
15. Write "ST MICHAEL PROTECT US" on five red tealights in the wax.
16. Dress each tealight with holy oil.
17. Set your fiery sword protection packet on the altar in a cross setup with one tealight on top of the packet and the 4 tealights at the cardinal directions.

The setup looks like a cross with your protection packet in the center.

18. Light the tealight in the center first which represents your spirit then light the candles from top to bottom and right to left. That's North, South, East, & West on a compass.

MIRROR PACKET

I've always worked with mirrors for fiery wall of protection work. Anytime you feel under attack or if those you love are in trouble you can place your names, photos, or petitions in a mirror packet and work that packet. Whoever is causing you trouble will feel the heat of their mess and will have to leave you alone.

There are several different ways I work a mirror packet. I will share with you one way that has worked very well for me and my clients over the years. I usually do this kind of work with White Eagle or the Holy Trinity but I will show you how to call Saint Michael for this work because he's a warrior. Anytime you feel like you are being wronged you can petition St Michael to protect you with his sword. That is one of the secrets to working with him. I've been online for several years and one thing I always notice is that online workers talk about asking Saint Michael for protection but they never mention calling his spirit to protect you with his sword.

Anytime you need protection call on St Michael to guard you from all sides then ask him to protect you with his fiery sword. You can use the sword of Saint Michael for cleansings, justice, protection, and enemy work.

Before you work with the mirrors you need to clean them in Salt water, ammonia diluted in water, or vinegar. Do not look or catch your reflection in those mirrors. You don't want to cross yourself up.

For this packet you'll need:

> Two small round mirrors,
> Red Cotton String,
> Hodgepodge or Elmer's glue,
> A red St Michael vigil candle,
> 9 white tealights,
> Isaiah 41 torn from the Bible,
> Devil's Shoestring,
> Bay Leaf,
> A small pinch of Sulfur,
> Five Finger Grass,
> Angelica Root,
> Master of the Woods,
> Calamus Root,
> Dragon's Blood (just a pinch).

This makes for total of nine ingredients which is Saint Michael's number. If you want to protect specific people you can include photos such as a photo of yourself and your loved ones but that is optional.

1. On Isaiah 41 write your name, the names of your family members, and any loved ones you want to include in this packet

2. Then write "ALL MY LOVED ONES" or "ALL THOSE I HOLD DEAR IN MY HEART"

This will provide a fiery wall of protection to everybody in your life even those you forgot to mention. When doing fiery wall you always want to include not only yourself but your family and those who care about you because when your enemies attack you or try to put you in a bind they'll go after your family if they can't harm you. When you include family in your protection work then troublemakers have no way of getting to you.

3. Write your personal petition on the Bible chapter
4. After you write the petition on *Isaiah 41* burn it to ash with the roots
5. Ask St Michael for protection as you burn the petition and roots because by burning your work to ash you are heating it up. This is the time to burn your photos to ash if you want to include that in your work. If you burn your roots until they're charred they'll be easier to grind when you make protection powder
6. Take the ash from your paper petition and roots then mix it in a mortar with Bay Leaf, Sulfur, Five Finger Grass, Master of the Woods, and Dragon's Blood
7. Grind with a pestle to a fine powder

Remember to stir your powder clockwise as you grind your herbs and roots.

8. State your petition for protection.
9. When the powder has reached a consistency you like, turn the round mirrors face down so the backs are exposed.

Make sure you don't look into those mirrors!

10. Sprinkle a thin layer of protection powder on the back of those mirrors.
11. Then spread a layer of hodgepodge or Elmer's glue over the powder till it's covered.

12. Then sprinkle a final layer of protection powder over the glue on both mirrors

Wait a little while just so the powder can settle in the glue but not too long because you don't want the glue to dry. If you need to add more glue because you didn't add enough when layering your work go right ahead. Save any leftover powder if you have it.

13. When the powder has settled in the glue after several minutes, press the backs of the mirrors against one another to make them stick

Make sure your mirrors are evenly pressed. The shiny sides of the mirrors should be facing out. The glue will hold your work together. The circle has no beginning or end. Nothing can get in or come out the circle. Nobody will be able to get through that. By doing your work this way you are building up your protection in layers.

14. Now take your red string and wrap it around your mirror packet towards you, turn it clockwise, then wrap towards you again until your packet is secure
15. Tie your packet off with nine knots

Your packet is complete. The last step is to work your Conjure packet.

16. Carve your name and ALL MY LOVED ONES in the wax of your St Michael vigil
17. Then over the names write:
    "The Lord is my Shepherd I shall not want..."
18. Dress the vigil with a little holy oil.
19. Sprinkle the leftover protection powder if you have any in a spiral from the edge of the candle to the center.
20. Hold the vigil close to your mouth and state your petition.
21. Say the revocation of Saint Michael and light the vigil.
22. Set the vigil on the mirror packet in the center.

23. Place nine white tealights around the mirror packet in a circle and light the candles clockwise starting from the East.
24. For the next eight days repeat the novena on the vigil for a total of nine days.
25. After nine days cover your mirror packet in a white handkerchief and hide it in a special place so no one can get to it.

If you are having ongoing trouble I recommend placing your packet under a statue of Saint Michael. Refresh your work at least once a week. You keep your work going by feeding the spirit. What I do in my personal practice is once a week, I redo the vigil candle and light it on my packet. I thank God and Saint Michael for protecting me during the week. Then I ask Saint Michael to lend his hand over me the following week. I pour a drop of Holy oil and Whiskey on his statue to heat him up so my protection will always be HOT to the touch!

Always keep in mind that anytime you work with mirrors never look directly into the mirror. If you came to my house and looked under my St Michael nine times out of ten you'll find many mirror packets neatly tucked under him. Saint Michael is one of my favorite saints. He has never failed me and can deliver justice like you could never imagine. I am glad to share this bit of information with you. I know it will help you just as it has helped many others.

SAINT LUCY THE LIGHT BRINGER

There's not a lot of information out there about St. Lucy. I've been working with her for a lot of years. St. Lucy's colors are white and only white! Her special day is December 13th and her altar holds 13 white flowers. Lucy means light. This is true because St. Lucy will shed light on any situation. She is also a good watcher to watch out for your enemies and with her eyes St Lucy will clear all confusion. Saint Lucy in her own right is a warrior saint and can be worked for darker work she can be petitioned for work to cross up your enemies. She is what is called a two-headed worker. She'll strip away whatever troubles are on you and at the same time knock those down that are trying to keep you from moving forward. St Lucy works like a double edged sword because she is a bringer of light and clarity to all situations where you are feeling depressed or low in your spirit. St. Lucy like St. Martha is also a good saint to petition when you have an unruly husband or unruly man. She is always on the side of the woman if there is a divorce; the woman will always have her way with St. Lucy.

St. Lucy is a patron saint of people who are blind and those who have eye troubles. This means not only that she will help with eye troubles but that if you are feeling confused Saint Lucy will remove the veil of confusion that has been placed over your eyes. Lucy is also a very powerful healer not just for eye problems. If you feel you have been crossed then go to St Lucy and ask her to clean you with her palm branch from the CROWN of your head (this where your spirit sits) to the bottom of your feet. The reason Saint Lucy is pictured holding a palm branch is because she was martyred for her undying faith in God.

The palm branch is a sign of faith in God and his power to be successful in all things. If you decide to setup an altar for St. Lucy you need to give her a pair of eyes in a white bowl. If you can't find a pair of eyes you can make these eyes out of clay and paint them white. Offerings to St. Lucy are white wine, powdered Sugar, Sugar, white flowers, white vigils, and a pair of eyes.

You can make a cleansing broom with the palm leaves; and the give the broom to Saint Lucy. When you have to do cleansing work you will work your Palm broom. To make a broom:

1. Bind a couple of palm leaves together using white ribbon
2. Find couple of good palm branches
3. Put them under cool running water and pray over them
4. Dress them with holy oil and lay a pinch of Salt on the palm broom
5. Let that sit overnight
6. Bless your palm broom by waving it in the sign of the cross over Frankincense and Myrrh

Anytime you are doing cleansings or healing work with Lucy you can petition her with the palm broom. You can decorate your St. Lucy broom however way you want but remember to only use white because that is her color. You can add white flowers, white roses, turtledoves for peace, and even a few dove feathers.

Since this is Saint Lucy's broom I recommend you glue a pair of eyes (especially blue eyes) to the broom so that Saint Lucy will always look out for you. What's really important is that you petition Saint Lucy to cleanse you and your loved ones with her palm broom. Tell her the broom is hers and you're giving it to her for her to work with. Call her spirit down into that broom.

1. Call her power and the power of God into a white handkerchief
2. Wrap the handkerchief around a photo of you and your loved ones burnt to ash
3. Add protection herbs, a bit of Devil's Shoestring, a silver dime, and a strong magnet into a packet

4. Remember to fold everything TOWARDS you until you can't fold anymore
5. Feed your packet a little Whiskey and holy oil to keep the power strong
6. Give the packet to St. Lucy for protection of you and yours

This does two things: (1) it makes the work stronger, and (2) it confuses the spirits. This is a lot of work but I promise you it is worth it because you are building up a power with God and Saint Lucy that can't be torn down. The Conjure palm broom for St. Lucy will remove crossed conditions from you when you sweep yourself from HEAD to TOE, sweeping away confusion and opening your eyes, reverse work back on your enemies. I love this broom because like Saint Lucy it works like a double edged sword.

Once your Conjure broom is done you need to offer it to Saint Lucy on her altar with:

A white vigil candle
A circle of white roses
A cup of Holy Water

1. Put your photo inside the glass of Holy Water with a pinch of kosher Salt
2. Write your name in the white vigil and dress it with holy oil
3. Light your vigil and petition God and Saint Lucy
4. Ask her to fill you with her light and to dispel the clouds of darkness in your life
5. Petition Saint Lucy to let you see everything clearly with eyes that are open!
6. Hold your hands over the glass of water and ask Saint Lucy again to make everything clear to you just like the glass of water

The water with your photo inside is an offering to Lucy. You are giving your spirit to God so his Prophet Lucy can fill you with her light.

7. Offer a little Frankincense and Myrrh incense
8. Dress the eyes of your broom with holy oil so your eyes will be open
9. And let your vigil burn
10. Every day for the next six days petition Saint Lucy to cleanse you, protect you and your loved ones, and fill you with peace and clarity. This will make a total of seven days

Each time you petition Lucy knock on her altar three times in the name of God the Father, Son, & Holy Ghost. I know this is a lot of work but the results are worth all the hard effort.

Now that you Conjure broom is ready you need to learn how to use it. There are many different ways to work a Conjure broom. Anytime you are feeling depressed, confused, or blocked you need to do a cleansing. To do a cleansing with Saint Lucy:

1. Knock on her altar three times to get her attention
2. Then starting at the CROWN of your head sweep yourself with the palm broom going DOWNWARD all the way to the bottom of your feet then go from heel to toe

Always remember to sweep yourself from HEAD to TOE. Do not go up and down or you will cross yourself up! Keep cleansing yourself with the broom until you feel like you are cleansed.

3. When I sweep myself I always do it three times in the name of the Holy Trinity. For each sweep over my body I say:

   "In the name of God the Father, God the Son, God the Holy Spirit I sweep all blocks, confusion, and crossed conditions away from me."

   This is the prayer I say but you must pray from your heart.

4. Once you're done sweeping with the broom then take a white tealight and cleanse yourself with the tealight just like you did with the broom from head to toe.

5. Place your photo under a statue of St. Lucy and light your tealight in front of the statue.
6. Pray your petition to Saint Lucy; and tell her you're placing yourself under her protection.
7. Stand your broom on her altar with the head of the broom up. This is important because as long as the broom is pointing up St Lucy will remove whatever is on you with that broom.
8. Now that you're cleansed you need to bless yourself so that your roads will always be open. For this part of the work you need to make a blessing oil for Saint Lucy. In a small bottle of Olive Oil add:

> Frankincense
> Myrrh
> Master of the Woods
> Eyebright Herb
> Angelica Root
> Sage

Master of the Woods will bring you power and total success. Angelica Root protects like a shield, and eye- bright will keep your eyes open so you can always see clearly what's ahead of you. This is important if you want to achieve success in your life. Sage will bring wisdom which is also pertinent to your success. Sage keeps you from getting confused too. Anytime someone throws a block on you they will confuse you. If you are confused then you can't move forward because you don't know what to do. I'm not just talking about work being thrown on you either but in general throughout life. When people are jealous of you and try to nail you down they don't want you to see the light at the end of the tunnel. The herb Sage with all the other ingredients will help you to find a way out of your bind and come out successful.

When you put all your ingredients into your oil:

9. Pray Psalm 23 into the bottle of oil

10. Petition God and Saint Lucy to fill your oil with power
11. Tell Saint Lucy the oil you made is for her to use
12. Check your oil with a pendulum to make sure the power is strong

The pendulum should move strong around the oil. If your pendulum doesn't move or slightly makes a pass then you need to keep praying over your oil until that pendulum moves like crazy. When your pendulum moves crazy then your oil is ready.

13. After your cleansing take a little of your St Lucy oil and dress yourself with it starting toe to heel coming upward your body

Make sure to dress your head. Petition St Lucy to give you strength and the upper hand in any situation you find yourself in; then just sit back and see what happens.

SAINT JUDE

Saint Jude is the saint of lost causes. We call upon him when we are in deep despair, he works the impossible. Some say you have to be careful with this saint; they say he will keep you in a bind so you will continue to call on him for help. This could be said just about any Saint or Spirit. The colors associated with Saint Jude are red, white and green. Sunday is the day of the week to start a petition to Saint Jude. Call on him at midnight the time between the darkest time of night and the morning light.

> Along with the advertisement in the news paper
> You need to offer him three shiny pennies
> Also give him a glass of water

To your altar you can add:

> A piece of broken chain; symbolizing that the chains that have kept you bound in misery has been broken
> Add a picture of yourself that was taken when you were very happy

Saint Jude will grant freedom to those who are locked away, either in jail or in their own minds. He is the Saint of freedom. If you are depressed and in deep despair:

1. Set up your altar and light a white candle to Saint Jude
2. Pray and pour your heart out to him and he will lift the darkness, so the light can come in
3. Ask him to break the chains that hold you down; to lift you up and set you free from the dark bounds that hold you. He will rescue you and set you free. Blessed be Saint Jude

Below is a novena to Saint Jude.

NOVENA TO SAINT JUDE

To Saint Jude, Holy Saint Jude, Apostle and Martyr, great in virtue and rich in miracles, near kinsman of Jesus Christ, faithful intercessor of all who invoke your special patronage in time of need. To you I have recourse from the depths of my heart and humbly beg to whom God has given such great power to come to my assistance. Help me in my present and urgent petition, in return I promise to make your name known and cause you to be invoked. Saint Jude pray for us and all who invoke your aid. Amen.

SAINT RAMON

Saint Ramon is a Spanish saint. He is used when you want to shut someone's mouth. If someone is harassing you and you want them to stop use San Ramon. Here's what you need.

San Ramon candle
1 penny
Persons name
Black marker
Powered herb that is used to shut people up

1. Light the candle once a bit of wax has melted get some on your finger and place it over the face of San Ramon, then stick the penny over the face
2. Write the person's name under the penny in a straight line down the glass
3. Then sprinkle the powdered herb in the candle and call on San Ramon to shut their mouth

Let the candle burn all the way out. This works fast within three hours of lighting the candle.

If you need to pay a bill you can petition San Ramon to help you pay your bill.

1. Set the bill on the table
2. Then set a red Saint Ramon candle on top of the bill
3. Set 4 green tea lights around the candle and light them
4. Call on Saint Ramon, and then light the red candle
5. Petition him to find a way to pay the bill

PROSPERITY CONJURE

You can petition San Roman for his help in all money matters. Start you work on Thursday. Set up a small space for San Ramon. Green and Red are his colors. Either have a statue or a photo of him on the altar. You need:

1. 3 nickels, [which you must never spend],
2. A Green Candle that you have written in the wax close to the wick:
   "The Lord is my Sheppard I shall not want"
3. Place a photo of yourself facing inward, so you can watch the flame burn
4. In a small glass of water place a bunch of Parsley
5. Pray and petition San Ramon to draw the money you need

Once a week pour the water on your front door stoop and throw the Parsley in the crossroads.

DIVINATION

In this section of the workbook you will find different methods of divination. You should be able to find something that will fit your spirit. We are not all blessed in the same way as we are all different. I can't read Tarot cards I never have been able too. I have about fifteen different decks. My spirit just doesn't understand them. So if you have a hard time with one reading tool you will find another one that works just as well. You should work with your ancestors when you are trying to "see" what is going on around you. They will share the information with you.

I CAN SEE CLEARLY NOW

You will be working with the Prophet Daniel. In Daniel 2 V 22 we see that God reveals things that are hidden.

"He reveals deep and secret things; He knows what is in the darkness, and light dwells with Him."

I've lived with the gift of sight my whole life; I have always just known things. I was never told that it was a sin or it was of the devil. I was never told it was evil. My mama had the sight, so did my Granddaddy and my Grandma on my daddy's side. The only person who ever said anything that someone might perceive as negative towards the gift was my other Grandma she said *"I was a heathen"*; which was probably true. I never had a bad experience in church or around church folk; my Mama wouldn't have put up with it.

I watched my mama many of times looking in a cup or a glass with water in it. Sometimes it was clear water sometimes it had a blue tint to it. I never asked her what she was doing. When she was in what we called "her Mood" we didn't mess with her. We just knew it was important. She never burned candles. I do because I love them.

When there is something hidden in the dark that you just can't put your finger on:

Get a jar or glass of water. J use an ole mason jar
Add a few drops of Ms. Stewart's bluing to the water
Along with a little Holy Water
Get a white stick candle and place it behind the jar
or glass

1. Petition God and the Prophet Daniel to help you find the answer you are looking for
2. Ask them to help you see what is hidden

I leave my jar on my table in my shop. I don't let the water dry up; if the water gets low I just add more water and stir it up. This is an ole school way of reading. If you haven't ever tried it you should.

PSYCHOMETRY

*P*sychometry is reading a person's spirit using their photo, name paper, hand writing, or any personal concerns. This is also accomplished by touching the client or being near them. In some ways when you do this you are touching a person's spirit. You can use psychometry to read a person, get into their head, and see what they're really up to. Conjure workers use psychometry all the time to discern people's motives and what they're really about. When we read a person this way we are actually picking up on the energy they hold. My Mama was very good at this. She could just look at a person and tell you about them. She had a very strong gift. I inherited my gift from her. I call it "reading a person's spirit". I can read a person by touching them, their voices or just by looking at them. I have found that the eye's of a person holds all their secrets. That is the first place I look when I meet someone. When I look at someone I just get a feeling about them, and the more I study them the more information I pick up.

If you're just starting in psychometry the best way to read a client or someone you know is by working with their photo.

1. Lay their photo on a table
2. Hold your pendulum over the photo
3. and call on their spirit to tell you the truth and show you what you need to see
4. Tell the pendulum to move when you are connected to their spirit. When the pendulum moves then you are in tune with their Spirit

Now you can start asking questions. If you got a High John root for a pendulum you can work that root around their photo if you want to dominate the person or make them do something.

To get a good read on a person you can petition La Madama to tell you everything you need to know.

1. Place their photo in front of your La Madama pot and call on her
2. Ask her to open your eyes and show you what's hidden
3. Then pray the Our Father and still your mind

You will hear her voice and when you do listen carefully. Whatever that person is hiding from you or whatever is going on in their lives will be known, you can also discover their intentions. If you have a strong relationship with La Madama then you can also look into her eyes and call out a person's name. La Madama will get her message across!

La Madama is wonderful for this type of work because she is the patron of readers. She will uncover what is hidden during a reading. La Madama was a powerful Conjure worker in her day, she speaks in a clear and understanding way. I have found that La Madama gives special favor to Conjure workers. She is a very strong spirit and when you work with her you feel her power and you hear her voice guiding you. She is perfect for this type of reading.

TRADITIONAL BONE READING

I have been reading bones in consultations with my clients for 25+ years. There is a lot of misconception about throwing the bones in Conjure. I was taught to read the bones by two different workers, one used possum bones and the other uses coon bones. They both prepare the bones in similar ways but not exactly the same. I learned both ways. I was taught that we are able to read the bones through our ancestors and the spirits that walk with us. You have to have a strong connection with your ancestors in order to receive the information through the bones. Your bones are very personal, and they should be taken care of after all this is a link between you and your ancestors. I was taught my bones are protected by my ancestors and if someone stole them they would have to deal with my ancestors. So I have no fear of taking a photo of my bones. All I can say is it sucks to be dumb if you are willing to go against someone's dead kin.

Traditional Conjure workers throw the bones to find out what ails their client. Therefore the client is present when the bones are thrown. I was taught to have the client stand on a white cloth then the bones are thrown in front of them on the floor while prayers are being said to find out what ails the client. There is more to this but this is all I am willing to share. Both workers gave the same instructions for reading a client. Once the reading is over the bones have to be cleansed and fed. Then they are place with the ancestors to be refreshed.

If I am doing a long distance reading for a client then I throw the bones on their photo. Sometimes I don't have to have a photo if I get a strong connection with them; the ancestors just speak through the bones. Reading the bones takes years to perfect, this is not something you can learn in a day or two. I am still learning after all these years of throwing the bones.

Above is a photo of a set of my bones I read during consultations. These are Traditional possum bones, I also have a set of coon bones that were fixed and given to me. The shell was given to me by MiMi who first taught me about the bones. It is used to move the bones around during the reading. I was taught not to touch them with my hands during a reading. The leather bag was made by my oldest son about thirteen years ago for my birthday to keep my bones in.

Each bone will represent something to the reader; I was taught that the ancestors name the bones for you. I have found this to be true. They guide you in understanding the mesSage. You will always have a bone that represents the ancestors and one that represents a male and a female. You should have a bone that is used to represent the client you are reading for. I have a buzzard bone that was given to me many years ago that I added to my bones, this bone lets me know if there is illness or blocks. It all depends on where the bone falls in the reading.

Bone throwing is becoming a thing of the past in Conjure as old workers are passing on. Folks are digging and scratching trying to find the information so it can be exploited on the net, so everyone and their brother can claim to be bone readers. If you are interested in learning to read the bones then get out and find an old Conjure worker to teach you. You have to be taught the basics hands on, this is not something you can just jump into or learn from a book or a few days of teaching. The bones have to be prepared before they are given to you. I have taught a few folks that are special to me or I feel spirit lead to teach to read the bones. I hold this information with a tight fist because I refuse to see it abused as so much information is being abused. Bone reading is the purest way to communicate with our ancestors to enrich our daily lives and the lives of our clients.

Working with La Madama

*L*a Madama is the spirit of an old slave who was a Conjure woman. She is the patron of card readers and rootworkers. She reads using a pack of playing cards and sometimes she holds a mirror while telling you all ya bizness!!! La Madama is a no nonsense spirit who'll tell it like it is to your face whether you like it or not. If you are a spiritual reader who's struggling with getting the truth out, call on La Madama because she'll sweep away all your troubles with her broom and bring the truth out ESPECIALLY if your clients are not being truthful with you or misleading you in any way.

Aunt Jemima is the image most often used to represent La Madama because of her skin color and the color of her clothes. If you look in the Bible you'll find that Jemima was the oldest and most beautiful of Job's three daughters. In the same book of Job you will find references to the signs that God put in our hands. It is no surprise then that Aunt Jemima of the Bible represents La Madama. There is obviously a link between La Madama and the Bible. You will find the reference to Jemima in Job 42: 14.

The colors associated with La Madama are red, white, and black. These colors derive from the color of her skin and the clothes she wears which is most often red and white. Most photos and statues of Aunt Jemima depict her with a broom which is most often associated with La Madama.

There are many tools spiritual workers employ when working with La Madama. The broom is one of the most important tools associated with her. She works with the broom to sweep out all crossed conditions, family issues, and troubles that clients may bring. Most card readers who work with La Madama house her in an iron pot with other tools such as a knife to nail down your enemies, a pack of playing cards to reveal all the client's troubles to the Conjure worker, a broom for cleansing and to sweep away

crossed conditions, some chalk to mark your work and lock it down, and a wooden cross to hold her power. These are the things most workers work with when calling on La Madama.

There are many works you can do with La Madama. She's not limited to one kind of work. I've called on her spirit to cleanse my clients, open their roads, or bring them total success in all they do. I've also seen La Madama settle down troublesome folks, bring money into the house, and help bills get paid on time. The list is endless of the things that La Madama can help you achieve especially since God gave her this power through Jemima when he restored Job. La Madama has the power to do these things because when God blessed Job they all began with Jemima his first-born.

The offerings La Madama accepts are Molasses, Whiskey, brown Sugar, a cool glass of water, and a vigil. She also likes to smoke cigarettes and sometimes will ask you for more! It'd be good if you buy her a pack of cigarettes for her to keep in her iron pot. Working with La Madama is Conjure Work at its finest! As an old slave Conjure woman La Madama chooses those who she'll work with...not the other way around! Being a Conjure woman La Madama carries the wisdom of all the old rootworkers from the past and by working with her you will have the knowledge, know how, and wisdom it takes to be a true spiritual worker. That's not to mention the "secrets" that La Madama shares with her closest children.

As a spirit of a Conjure woman who sees all things La Madama is not only a card reader but a bone reader. Some spiritual workers throw the bones before La Madama when they need immediate answers. Through her bones she tells the Conjure worker what to do and how to get the job done. Her connection to the bones and bone reading is a link to her past on the African continent. As you can see La Madama is an old spirit worker who can do many things to assist you in your daily life like she helped her father Job in the Bible. Conjure workers do not limit themselves to certain kinds of work with her because La Madama can do it all!

BIBLIOMANCY

*T*he Bible is the most powerful book in Conjure! You can get answers to all your questions by working with your Bible or use what some folks call Bibliomancy. To begin working with the Bible hold it in your hands and ask God to show you all the answers you need in a way that you'll understand. When you ready open your Bible and read the first verse that your eyes fall on. If you don't get your answer then you may have to read a little further.

A lot of old Conjure workers use this technique to find answers in order to help their clients. You can also use the key as a pendulum when working with your Bible. The key belongs to St Peter because God give him the keys to heaven and earth. When you find the verse you are led to hold your key over it and ask God if that verse is the answer to your question. If the answer is no then close the Bible and ask your question again. Repeat the process until you find the answers you seek.

As a part of working with your Bible you can use a person's photo. Look into their eyes and ask God to open your eyes about the person. Hold your Bible in your hands and ask your question. Open the Bible at random and the first verse you see will show that answer. If the person needs prayer you can place that photo in the Bible where you got your answer. If Spirit shows that the person is bad for you turn their photo upside down and place it in the Bible facing the verse. Ask God to turn the person's life upside down and reverse everything they do against you back onto them.

SLAM your Bible as hard as you can and call for justice! If through Bible divination you determine that the person you're reading is confused or needs healing work done open your Bible to (give verses for healing/cleansing work) and place their photo on top of those verses. Everyday say the person's name and read that verse.

If you don't know the right prayers to say when working with your Bible then say the Prayer of Daniel to Uncover the Truth & Open Your Eyes.

The Prayer of Daniel
(Daniel 2: 20-23)

Blessed by the name of God forever and ever:
For wisdom and might are his:
And he changeth the times and the seasons:
he removeth kings, and setteth up kings:
he giveth wisdom unto the wise,
and Knowledge to them that know understanding.
He revealeth the deep and secret things:
He knoweth what is in the darkness,
and the light dwelleth with him.
I thank thee, and praise thee,
O thou God of my Fathers,
who hast given me wisdom and might,
and hast made known unto me
now what we desired of thee:
for thou hast now made known unto us
the king's matters *(or you can say all matters)*.
Amen.

When done with your consultation thank God for showing you the truth and ask him to keep your eyes open at all times.

CARD READING

*M*inor Arcana — show specific people, their intentions based on the suit, and personalities. Compare with the suits of regular playing cards.

Cups — Hearts (love, home, family, ancestry, lineage, children, youth)

Spades — Swords (obstacles, blockages, delays, setbacks, issues with the law and government, health issues)

Clubs — Wands (work, employment, how far you're willing to go to achieve)

Diamonds — Coins (Money, finances, business prospects, hard work, how you appear to the world)

Ace of Diamonds — means money, wealth, fame because of your hard work. The Ace of Diamonds shows the easy route to fame and riches. This card represents money, accomplishments, and is an all-around good card. Represents total success.

If you get more red cards then the outcome is positive. Red cards are "alive" and full of life. Black cards show a negative outcome.

Ace of Spades — death of a relationship, death of a person, ending of business venture, a major block that's persistent and holds you down. When you get this card reconsider your options. From a hoodoo Conjure point of view you need to do a major uncrossing.

Ace of Clubs — positive movement towards people and work, moving up to success in life. An all-around good luck card. Focuses on money, professional life, and your career.

Ace of Hearts — a love and marriage card. If this comes up then a proposal will come about. It also represents the state of a person's marriage. If you have an Ace of Hearts with Spades and Clubs around it then there's a problem with your marriage.

For Love Work Use:

The Ace of Hearts
9 of Hearts
The card representing the one you want

1. Name the card for the person. Buy a new deck of playing cards just for work. Once the work's over clean your deck of cards
2. Set the 3 cards on a red plate in a line
3. Place their photo over the card that represents them
4. Around the cards and the photo sprinkle a mixture of:
   Damiana
   Powdered Pyrite
   Lodestone grit
   Master of the Woods
   Calamus

5. Set your vigil on top of the card that represents the person and the person's photo
6. Outside of the plate set up 4 tealights in the shape of a cross
7. Pray and state your petition that you want the person to come.

To Separate Two People:

1. Place the Ace of Spades between two cards representing them on a round black plate
2. Place the photo representing each person on top of their card
3. Sprinkle a mix of:
   Red Pepper
   Sulfur
   Dirt Daubers Nest
   Crossroads dirt over the cards

4. State your petition
5. Place a black Break Up candle on the Ace of Spades
6. Light it, and state your petition

For Money Work:

Place a 9 of Hearts
Ace of Diamonds
Ace of Clubs
5 of Diamonds in the shape of a cross
Your personal card and photo in the center

The 5 of Diamonds draws money to you and the 9 of Hearts is the happiest card in the deck.

1. Put a purple vigil in the center.
2. Make a mixture of 5 herbs that bring money and power.
3. Sprinkle the mixture around your vigil, card, and photo in the center to nail down your work.
4. Inside your vigil write your name closest to the glass.
5. Then going towards the center write
   "The Lord is my Shepherd I shall not want..."

It doesn't matter if you can't see the words.

6. Dress and bless your vigil then light it.
7. On each of the 4 cards on the outside light a tealight while stating your petition of what you want.

Go daily and state your petition over your work.

THE PENDULUM

A pendulum is a tool that tells you the truth about folks and what's going on. Most workers use the pendulum for yes and no answers but you can make an alphabet board and get full sentences by using the pendulum. In this section of the book we will tell you how to make your own pendulum, how to use one, and how to make an alphabet board. One of the most famous Conjure pendulums is made with a Queen Elizabeth root and red string.

Did you know that you can clean your pendulum in coffee grounds? You can leave it in there for 24 hours and it will be ready to work. What the coffee grounds do is remove blocks and negative energy from the pendulum. You can also use running water or Salt.

TO BLESS YOUR PENDULUM:

1. Dress it with Holy Oil or Special Oil #20.
2. Make the sign of the cross with your pendulum
3. Call on Spirit to always lead you to the truth and the right answers

You can use anything for a pendulum but what I found is that a key, a cross, a mercury dime, a black cat vertebrae, and a spiritual medal are the best items to use other than a Queen Elizabeth root. You can also use a Rosary for a pendulum. The cross represents the crossroads where all information is received. The key is used because St Peter holds the keys which opens the way to your intuition. All that is received through St Peter will be automatically received in Heaven. You can see in Isaiah and the Book of Matthew that God gave St. Peter the keys to heaven.

Isaiah 22 V 22-23

> *22 And the key of the house of David will I lay upon his shoulder; so he shall open, and none shall shut; and he shall shut, and none shall open.*
>
> *23 And I will fasten him as a nail in a sure place; and he shall be for a glorious throne to his father's house.*

Matthew 16:18-19

> *18 And I say also unto thee, That thou art Peter, and upon this rock I will build my church; and the gates of hell shall not prevail against it.*
>
> *19 And I will give unto thee the keys of the kingdom of heaven: and whatsoever thou shalt bind on earth shall be bound in heaven: and whatsoever thou shalt loose on earth shall be loosed in heaven.*

The Mercury dime can be used because of its protective qualities. Silver also draws which will draw your intuition. A black cat bone is lucky because everybody knows cats have a psychic sense so what better way to find answers by using a black cat vertebrae?

The pendulum is often used in Conjure work to determine if a job will be successful. The best way to train your pendulum is to give you yes and no answers. Tell your pendulum to move for yes and stop for no because it's quite confusing when you try to work with the pendulum the way most people talk about working with it. Keep it simple. Working with the pendulum does not have to be hard.

For a pendulum you can also use a John the Conqueror root because it will remove all obstacles standing in your way that's blocking your intuition and it will open the way for your second sight to come in clear. To make the John the Conqueror pendulum you need to drill a small hole in the root and run your red string through the hole. The root is so hard it's easy to drill a hole in it.

You can also use an Angelica Root as a pendulum because as we all know the Angelica Root belongs to the angels. You can dedicate the root to St. Michael and ask him to protect you. Wear your Angelica Root everywhere you go. Anytime you have trouble the Angelica Root will tell you.

If you work with the saints you can get a medal belonging to the saint you work closely with and dedicate that medal to the saint in the form of a pendulum. Dress and bless the medal and pray the saint's novena over the metal letting your breath touch the medal.

One of the ways I was taught to use a pendulum other than getting answers is to check if a client is blocked or not.

1. Dress and bless the client's hand by making the sign of the cross with Holy Oil over the palm of the hand
2. Call on the person's spiritual protector and ask them to please show you through the pendulum if the client is blocked or not
3. Hold the pendulum over the center of the client's hand
4. Bless the client in the name of the Holy Trinity
5. Then say:

   "I call on the spiritual protector of so-and-so. I ask that you give me a true and honest reading and show me any blocks on so-and-so."

If there are any blocks the pendulum will not move. If there are not any blocks the pendulum will move strong and hard.

If you made a High John pendulum you can use that pendulum on a photo to reverse whatever blocks are on you or your client. Spin the High John root over the name or photo going counterclockwise to remove while praying that all blocks are removed and destroyed.

TO MAKE AN ALPHABET BOARD:

1. Make 26 squares for each letter of the alphabet on a piece of paper
2. In each square write the letters of the alphabet from A to Z

When you get ready to use the alphabet the next step is time consuming but in the end result it's well worth it because you can get dates, names, places, and full sentences.

3. Lay your board out and call on the Spirit so you may get true and honest answers you need
4. Ask your question then hold your pendulum over the first letter which is A and then say:

   "Show me the truth. Is this the first letter in the first word which will answer my question?"

   If the pendulum moves then that's YES then you write the A down on your paper. If the pendulum doesn't move then the answer is NO and you move on to the next letter.

5. Continue this process until you have the answer that you're looking for

As you can see the pendulum is a powerful tool. It's used for more than just yes and no answers.

Automatic Writing

Before you begin automatic writing MAKE SURE you are strongly protected because you are inviting the spirit in. Automatic writing is different from any other divination because you are allowing the spirit to make personal contact with you and speak through you.

I learned to do automatic writing when I was in my early teens. I used to just sit in my bedroom, clear my mind, draw, and write with pen and paper. If you decide to work with automatic writing you need to buy a new tablet and a new pen. You'll only use these tools for automatic writing and nothing else.

Before you start an automatic writing session you need to spiritually cleanse yourself and call on St Michael to put a fiery wall of protection around you. You need to have a white or a blue taper candle that you've dressed with Fiery Wall of Protection oil and dress yourself. Get your tablet and pen and turn out the lights. Light your taper and call on your ancestors and the spirits that help you communicate. Pick up your pen, set it on top of your paper, and watch the flame of the taper burn for a little while and clear your mind. Once the spirit gets on you start writing. Your mind has to be clear of everything in order to be able to do this. Don't worry about what you're writing. Stay focused on the movement of the flame and let the spirit speak through your hands.

Once your hands start moving you'll know that the spirit is there so that you can start asking questions. Don't speak the questions out loud. Just let the questions run over and over and over in your mind. You will receive the answer. Once you're done you need to snuff out your candle and save it for a later date then you can look at what you wrote and see if it makes sense. One important thing to remember is that when you start this you ask Spirit to give you true and honest answers. Interpret what you have written.

It make take a few tries before you do this because most of the time our minds don't want to settle down and clear to do this type of work. If you find it difficult to do this work just keep trying over and over until you succeed. Keep your tablet as a diary. The more you do this the more your work will improve. After a while it will be simple for you to just light your candle, pick up your pen, and you'll automatically start writing.

Some folks are afraid of automatic writing because in order to achieve what I call "the zone" you have to let your guards down and open your spirit up. This makes some folks very nervous and therefore they are unable to succeed in automatic writing. If you have a specific spirit that you work with whether it be your ancestors or another spirit like La Madama you can call on them. Since La Madama is known for her divination skills you can petition her when you are doing automatic hand writing.

You can petition La Madama to open the veil so you can get the answers you are seeking. To do this:

1. Light a red vigil in her iron pot and offer her a smoke
2. Before you light the candle knock three times on the floor with her walking stick and call La Madama
3. Then light her candle
4. Give her a small cup of Molasses, brown Sugar, and Whiskey mixed together
5 Tell her this offering with the smoke and the candle is her payment for helping you see things clearly

You can do this work anytime you are confused and need clear honest answers. I've worked with La Madama for several years and I can tell you personally that she is one spirit that doesn't play around!!!

She gets straight to the point and is a tell it all kind of girl!!! If she gets too blunt don't take it personal because that is the way she is and the very reason why Conjure workers work with her. She'll set you right and put you on the straight and narrow path.

When done with your automatic writing thank La Madama and ask her to close the door. Then thank St. Michael and ask him to always watch your back. Offer St. Michael a white or red tealight with a fresh glass of cool water for his offering.

SCRYING

*B*efore you scry you need to:

1. Cleanse yourself, clear your mind, and get into "the zone"
2. Don't forget to protect yourself and call on St. Michael so that he's watching you with his fiery sword of protection
3. Ask the Holy Spirit to give you guidance and insight on the right thing to do

You can use anything to scry like a cup of water, a candle flame, a crystal ball, or a mirror to scry.

4. Write your name on a white taper candle
5. Dress it with Special Oil #20
6. Light the candle
7. Pray *Psalm 23*
8. Ask God to open your eyes so you may see clearly and protect you
9. Place your tool in front of you whether it be a crystal ball, mirror, or candle and look into that tool with your vision out of focus

At first you might not see anything but keep trying because you will have results. With you tool you may see faces, shapes, or places regardless of what you're using.

As you get "into the zone" you'll see smoke in the tool you're using. This is a good sign that spirit is opening your eyes. As you gaze into your tool you will start to see faces, letters, and people. These people may be spirits around you or actual people you know. If you petitioned Spirit about a specific person then you'll see that person and everything around them. When you get stronger into the works it will seem like you are standing next to the people you're looking.

To See What a Person's Doing:

1. Write their name in the wax of a white vigil
2. Call on their spiritual protector to let you see what's going on with them
3. Light the vigil
4. Sit back
5. Watch the flame while you are focused on the person who you're burning the vigil on

If the flame is small then you know that the person's spiritual protector is trying to protect them so you can't see what they're doing. You are now in a battle.

6. You have to keep demanding that you be let in

Once the walls are down the flame will get larger and start moving.

7. Focus on the person and let Spirit talk to you so you'll know what that person is doing. You will see either through the flame of the vigil or by smoke on the glass of the vigil what that person is up to
8. Let the vigil burn continuously throughout the week and as it burns watch the flame closely
9. If you see black smoke then that means the person is hiding something from you or is bad for your spirit in some kind of way
10. Watch the wax of the vigil and the glass for signs like letters, numbers, and the shape of the wax on the glass

These signs will tell you the truth.

Working by the Clock

I was not taught to work by the moon phases, in my family that was considered witchcraft which was a sin and went against God. I was raised in the Pentecostal church, so moon phases didn't have a place in my life other than when to cut my hair, when to plant or when to remove a wart and such. I don't mean any disrespect to anyone or how they believe; but since this is my book and my writings I feel like I have the right to speak plain. At a young age I was lucky to meet an old Conjure worker, she explained to me about working by the clock. She told me she didn't have time to wait for the moon to settle. I have to agree with her. When I have a job to do I don't wait on the moon; the work comes out just as good working by the clock.

This information is being lost like a lot of the other old ways because folks don't know about it. When you work by the clock you work to remove something when the hand on the clock is going downward. So if I wanted to do a reversal work you would start that work at around five minutes after midnight. You can start the work at any time after the hour but I like midnight because that is a very powerful time.

Now if I am going to take a cleansing bath I will start the bath at around twenty after the hour, this gives me ten minutes in the tub before the hand starts moving upward. By the time the hands are moving upward towards the next hour I am dried off and have dressed myself with Conjure Oil. I dress from toes to heal and upward. This is done to draw things to me. Get the idea? Try this and you will see once you get the hang of it you will never wait for a moon phase again to do your Conjure work.

I do try to work with the days of the week and the planets; but if I have a job that has to be done and it is not on the right day I will still do the work. I was taught not to let anything stop me from doing my work and I have always lived by that with great success.

Sometimes a work might take a while but I just keep hitting it until it is done. Here is a little money vigil trick that you should try it works really well.

1. Get a seven day green vigil
2. At 11:35 am start dressing your vigil and get it ready to light
3. Say your prayers and do whatever you do to get your vigils ready
4. Now at 11:45 tap the candle three times and on each tap say:

    "the Lord is my Sheppard and I shall not want".

5. Then light your vigil
6. At noon say your petition over your vigil
7. Then every day at noon until the candle burns out go to your space and say your prayers and your petition

Try this I think you will see a difference in your money work.

Have you ever wondered where the old sayings began? Like the one that goes:

"I worked my fingers to the bone from morning (am) noon and night (pm)".

Or how about the one that goes:

"I work from dusk till dawn with only time to pray at noon"

If we paid more attention to the ole sayings that ole folks say we might actually learn something. How about this one:

"I pray morning (am) noon and night (pm)"

These sayings started somewhere; and some smart ole Rootworker put them to good use.

There are certain times of the day that hold more power than other times during the day. The ole folks know this. I have been blessed with this knowledge and I am going to share it with you. This is something that shouldn't be lost but it will be if it is not passed on.

You don't find much about it on the internet because folks don't know about it; they haven't been told or it would be on every Conjure website you click on. I am going to try to explain it the way it was explained to me. I hope I don't botch the explanation.

6am; the sun rises after a long nights sleep; empowered by its rest the sun is ready to bring its light too us.

The key words here are (brings it light to us). This tells us that when the sun rises it is a time to work to bring things into our lives. This is the time for money work and success work.

12 noon; or high noon as my Grandma used to say. This is the time when the sun is its most powerful. Any work that is done at this time is sure to be a success. This is the time for money work or anything you want to draw to you.

6pm; this is the time when the sun has done its job all day and it is time to rest. The key words here are (the job is done). So any work that you started on that morning should be put to rest until the next morning when the sun rises. Then you can begin your work again.

What about the ole saying:

"I worked from dusk till dawn with only time to pray at noon"

I have to be honest this stumped me.

There is no noon between dusk and dawn; but there is a midnight which is the number 12 on the clock. When the sun is high it is at its most powerful, so when the clock strikes 12 midnight this time of night is at its most powerful hour.

6(pm); dusk is when the sun is going down, this is the time when we do work to remove things from us. If you are doing a reversal work this would be the time to start the work.

12 (am midnight) this is the most powerful time of the night; at this time you would have success in any kind of work to remove something or someone from you.

6(am) this is the time when you put to rest the work you started the night before. You wait until dusk the next day to pick the work up again.

When I burn a candle for Conjure work by the hour; meaning at 6 am, noon, and 6 pm. I work with what I have always called large stick candles; most of you call them jumbo candles. You will need something to mark your candle with, and to dig a hole, either in the side of the candle or in the bottom of the candle. Save the wax that you removed because once you load your candle you need to plug the hole back up. I use a large nail.

The first thing you need to do is mark your candle off in sections that will burn for about fifteen minutes each.

When I work with this type of candle in my Conjure work I always set the candle in a bowl; I do this not only for safety but also so I can add things to the work that will add more power. You don't have to do this you can just burn the candle if that is the way you work. Below you will find an example of how this works. There will be more later on in the book.

Money Drawing

For this Conjure work we will be working in the AM hours of the day' the reason for this is because we want to bring something into our lives.

1. When you are working in the AM you light your candle and start the work at about a quarter till 6 am
2. Let your candle burn until 6 am then snuff your candle out
3. At a quarter till twelve you relight your candle and let it burn until noon the snuff the candle out
4. Again at a quarter till 6pm you light your candle and then at 6pm you snuff the candle out

You work this process daily until the candle has burned completely.

I always try to start this work on Thursday or Friday, but if I have a need to do this type of Conjure then I start it on any day of the week.

I was taught not to set limits on my work, if I have a job to do then I just do the job and KNOW that it will be a success. When we set limits in Conjure work then we are holding our own selves back from being successful workers. I know that it seems like burning a candle this way is a lot of work; but the benefits are well worth the work you have to put into it. Besides nothing is free in this life; you have to give something in order to get something.

REVERSAL WORK

For this work you need:

> A black seven day candle
> Your Bible

1. Call on the Trinity; God the Father, God the Son, and God the Holy Spirit
2. Began wiping yourself going downward from the crown of your head to the bottom of your feet with the candle
3. While you pray *Isaiah 3 V 10-18*
4. Light the candle, let it burn for twenty-four hours
5. Then go daily three times a-day when the hand on the clock is moving downward and pray your petition and V 10-18 over the candle

When you are doing reversal or cleansing work you shouldn't feed the candle oils and powders. If the candle is full of spiritual food it can't eat away at what is hold onto to your spirit; so don't feed this type of candle. As the candle burns the crossed condition burns away.

Isaiah 3 V 10-18.

> *10 Say ye to the righteous, that it shall be well with him: for they shall eat the fruit of their doings.*
>
> *11 Woe unto the wicked! it shall be ill with him: for the reward of his hands shall be given him.*
>
> *12 As for my people, children are their oppressors, and women rule over them. O my people, they which lead thee cause thee to err, and destroy the way of thy paths.*
>
> *13 The LORD standeth up to plead, and standeth to judge the people.*
>
> *14 The LORD will enter into judgment with the ancients of his people, and the princes thereof:*

for ye have eaten up the vineyard; the spoil of
the poor is in your houses.

15 What mean ye that ye beat my people to pieces,
and grind the faces of the poor? saith the Lord
GOD of hosts.

16 Moreover the LORD saith, Because the
daughters of Zion are haughty, and walk with
stretched forth necks and wanton eyes, walking
and mincing as they go, and making a tinkling
with their feet:

17 Therefore the LORD will smite with a scab the
crown of the head of the daughters of Zion, and
the LORD will discover their secret parts.

18 In that day the Lord will take away the bravery
of their tinkling ornaments about their feet, and
their cauls, and their round tires like the moon,

WORKING WITH THE SPIRIT

When you hear folks talking about working with a spirit it means exactly that; you call on a spirit to work with you and ask the spirit to help you in whatever type of work you are doing. Just because you call on a spirit you have chosen to work with doesn't mean that spirit will answer your call! Spirit chooses who they will work with not the other way around. I think there is a big misconception out there about working with spirit. I also think that some folks abuse the gift of power that spirit gives us. When some folks get a touch of power they go nuts. They think they can rule the world and it is all about them about how powerful they are. Often times they tend to forget where the power for success in the work truly comes from. We as people have personal power but it will NEVER be as strong as spirit! When we start thinking we are all powerful we are headed for trouble.

I was taught that if a spirit chooses to work with you that the spirit will do the job as long as it is justified; they will not take it upon themselves to do whatever they want to. What I mean by this is they want work on your behalf without you asking for help. Unless you are working with dark spirit's and can't control them. These spirits are better left alone unless you know what you are doing; even then they should be left alone. There is really no way to control a spirit as far as I am concerned. They are far more powerful than you think you are. They are very powerful and really could care less what happens to us humans. They will not only cause the person harm you are working on but they will also turn on you if you can't control them. I have seen this happen with some workers. Then they start yelling that someone has crossed them up when they opened the door themselves. They fool themselves into thinking they are all powerful and in total control; when in reality the spirit is in control!

It is much safer to work with your ancestor's, or the Saint's. Even then you need to be careful. But I have found that these are the safest spirit's to work with. I think that a lot of folks throw caution to the wind to achieve what they want. I can't express how unsafe this type of thinking is. You can't just call on any ole spirit because you read about it or someone told you about it. The spirit chooses who they will work with and just because they work with one person doesn't mean they will work for another the same way. Please don't let your hunger for power over ride good sense! Always use your common sense when doing this type of work.

You must always remember that you have to protect yourself while doing this type of work. You can't just say one day "Oh I think I will call on some spirits"; no pun intended. You must use safety; Even if you are working with your ancestors. You have to remember when working with your ancestors that the spirit doesn't change. The body maybe gone but their spirit is still the same. If they were a horrible person when they were alive they are still horrible. Just because they passed on doesn't make them a saint. I must also caution you about working with a spirit you know nothing about. I don't think it's safe. Sometimes it's not safe to work with our own ancestors. I can't stress this enough. I know there is a lot of information out there on the internet but just because someone wrote it doesn't mean it is the right thing to do.

Two years ago a fella came to me needing a cleansing. He was in bad shape. I'm not going to tell you everything but I will point out the high points of how he got into the situation he found himself in. Sometimes it is not safe for us to work with our own ancestors. If you have an ancestor who hated you in life; then just because they have passed doesn't mean their feelings for you have changed. Also too many people take graveyard work lightly. They THINK they know what they are doing until they get a spirit on them that they can't get off. That is basically what happened to this fella. This spirit who was one of his ancestors was literately sucking the life out of him. Every facet of his life was in the crapper.

If it seems like I'm hiding something in this story I'm not. This fella is a well-known Conjure worker and I want put all his business out there. But this needs to be told so you understand how dangerous working with spirit can be! He has two relatives buried side by side. One was very hateful and abusive in life; while the other one was very caring and loving. For whatever reason he started doing graveyard work; because of the situation he got into I know he didn't have a lot of experience. On further speaking with him I knew for sure he was very inexperienced for this type of work. Basically what happened was he went to the graveyard to work with the loving relative and left himself wide open for the other relative to attach their spirit to him. In other words he brought a violent spirit home with him.

It took a lot of work to get that spirit off of him. I ended up getting hurt in the process in more ways than one. I warned him then not to do any more graveyard work. I was taught that once you get a spirit like that on you; then the next time it is easier for them to get to you. I don't think he followed my advice because I heard he is in bad shape again. Like him when things like this happen the first thing folks want to do is blame others. They think that folks are throwing at them when they opened the door themselves. I just don't understand why folks throw caution and safety to the wind. There is too much information out there now days and not enough hands on training; this is very dangerous!

Too many folks just jump right into this type of work without any training. They think because they have read about it, studied it, someone they hold in high regard has wrote about it; that it's ok to jump in with both feet.

Spirits of the dead are nothing to play around with. The information on how to work with the spirits use to be hush hushed. You surely didn't read about it. Now it is everywhere you look! People giving folks instruction on how to gather graveyard dirt, telling folks to work with dead folks they don't know, giving folks instruction on how to work with the Intranquil spirit; which is a very dangerous spirit! This type of work is not something you just jump into; you need to have help at first.

First let's talk about working with dead folks you DON'T know. You don't have a clue what type of person you are dealing with for starters. You don't know how they lived their lives. You don't have a clue; they could be anything from a murderer that didn't get caught, to a child molester who got away with it. Do you really think it is safe to bring a spirit you don't know into your life? I'm mean really! Here's an example of one everyone seems to think it is ok to work with. A soldier; why because they are made to follow orders; I think that is a bunch of hog wash! You don't have a clue what that soldier was really like in life. Did you do a military back ground check on him before you decided to disturb his spirit?

Just because someone was a soldier doesn't mean they followed orders! It doesn't mean they will do what you ORDER them to do! You don't have a clue as to what type of person you are dealing with! Soldiers are brain-washed into following orders and doing what they are told. I'll give you that; but not every person who is in the military is stable.

Not all of them are good soldiers. We hear it on the news all the time. So how do you really know that you picked a good soldier to work with? There's no way you can know! Come on folk's use your common sense God gave you here. I'll ask you again; how do you know that you have a good soldier to work with? You don't! There is no way for you to know unless it is a family member that you know. Even then you can't be sure they will follow your orders.

If you feel that you just have to do graveyard work then please work with folks you know. I'm not saying that all unknown spirits are unsafe to work with; but really why take the chance? There is nothing that your ancestors can't help you with. There is really no need to work with a graveyard spirit you know nothing about. I think in this day and age we have forgotten that we need to respect our dead. I am not by any means against graveyard work. I work a lot with the dead. What I do have a problem with; is folks who don't have a clue what they are doing and just jump right in with both feet. This is dangerous! Then when they get into trouble they start hollering everybody and their brother is throwing at them. I have a big issue with this.

"My Mama always told us; the dead can't hurt
you but they can make you hurt yourself"!

The Intranquil spirit seems to be the hottest spirit around for love work. Are you crazy? Do you even know what type of spirit you are dealing with when you call on the Intanquil spirit? Talk about playing Russian roulette with your life! I know that over half the folks that are advised to contact this spirit doesn't have a clue what they are doing or they wouldn't be doing it! I'm going to be blunt here and I don't apologize for it! If I step on toes; oh well I'm sorry for your luck! Most folks who work with this spirit are women who are trying to get their men back. They are desperate.

In their desperation to get their man back they are willing to do anything; even work with a very dangerous spirit. Why would they do such a thing? Well for one thing I don't think that they are well informed on just what the Intranquil spirit is. Another thing is that there are some out there that encourage folks to work with this spirit. They do this by stating how powerful this spirit is and how the spirit will stay on the person until they do what they are told to do. What they FAIL to tell these folks is; that this spirit can literally suck the life out of the person you have sent the spirit after. Not only that but this spirit can and will turn on you. Folks are under a misconception about the Intranquil spirit. Most folks think the Intranquil spirit is just one spirit. You are so very wrong!

When you call on the Intranquil spirit it is like opening up a box of cracker jacks you don't know what the prize will be! You see the words Intranquil Spirit are deceiving in its self. It gives us the impression that we are calling on one spirit. This is absolutely not true! The Intranquil spirit is ANY unhappy spirit wondering around out there. It is not just one single spirit. These spirits could have been killers, rapist, drug addicts, alcoholics, folks who committed suicide; they are dark spirits who have no peace.

Do you really think that anything is worth calling this type of spirit into your life? I mean come on folks; where is your common sense? Why in the world would you take a chance with a spirit like this? I know how desperate some folks can get; but working with this type of spirit is not the answer.

They say that these spirits will work for a glass of water; this may be true but what happens when the glass of water is not enough? What happens when this spirit attaches itself to you and you start wanting alcohol or you start wanting to do things you have never done before?

Please don't fool yourself into thinking it can't happen because it can! These spirits that make up the Intranquil spirit are desperate, they're hurting, lonely and they are miserable. Why in the world would you even think about contacting a spirit like this? Do you realize that you are sending this spirit out after someone you claim to love! Who in their right mind would send a spirit out whose prayer begins;

"O, Intranquil Spirit, you that in Hell are wandering and will never reach Heaven, hear me, o, hear me."

You are basically calling a demon to come to you. There are other ways to get a lover back without calling on the Intanquil spirit.

Since most folks learn to work from books and information they find on-line they are not taught how important it is to protect yourself before you do any type of spiritual work. I found very little on how to protect you; what I did find was a lot of information on love work, enemy work, graveyard work and such. That's all good and fine but you need to be protected before you go jumping into all these jobs! That is the problem with all this information being out there; it is in pieces. It is used to fill up books and web pages and if it is there it's in a completely differ section of the website. Folks need to take responsibility for the information they put out there! Before you do any type of spiritual work you need to have personal protection up. Here are the steps you should take when you decide to do a job.

PROTECTION FIRST

This is a must; when you work you draw all kinds of ugliness to you. All spirits are drawn to the energy we put out when we work. Why in the world would you not protect yourself? Please think before you act; use your good sense god gave you.

THE CROSSROADS SPIRIT

A crossroad is any road where two roads cross. There is a lot of magic in a crossroads, it is said that the crossroads is a place without time. One thing is for sure *"the crossroads is a place of power"*. Over the years there have been many stories about the crossroads. In rural towns in the South there are a lot of folks who want be caught at the crossroads at dark; even in this day and age. Many folks grew up on stories of the Black man who owns the crossroads; some even say he is the devil but I like to call him the crossroads spirit.

I use the symbol of the crossroads on my petition papers sometimes but it never can replace a real crossroads in power. I think that in order to ask a favor you must go to the crossroads. Working with the crossroads is not only limited to some dirt gathered from the four corners but also in our actions. For example every time you work with the cross you are calling on the crossroads. When you make the sign of the cross in the name of the Holy Trinity you are working with the crossroads. Anytime you use a cross in your Conjure work you are working with the crossroads. You can work with the crossroads to bring something to you or remove something away from you. It all depends on the work you're doing.

I myself have felt the power of the crossroads when I went there for help with my writing skills. It was a calm clear night; and no I didn't see the man but a breeze did pick up and I saw a mist in the center of the crossroads. My writing did improve; I now have three books written. Some say it is an old wives tale but I felt the power. Powerful Conjure work can be achieved at the crossroads. I petition the keeper of the crossroads often on behave of myself and my clients.

A simple but effective way to do this is to:

1. Collect a little dirt from each corner of the crossroads
2. Leave three pennies on each corner as payment for the dirt
3. Take the dirt back to your work space
4. Write your petition out and burn the petition to ash
5. Mix the ash with the dirt from the crossroads you collected
6. Dress a candle and sit it in the center of your dirt
7. Say your prayers and state your petition
8. Light the candle and let it burn all the way down
9. Once the candle has gone out gather up the dirt and any candle that is left
10. To this add three pennies
11. Go back to the crossroads and state your petition; throw everything in the center of the crossroads

Go home and KNOW that your petition will be answered.

TO REMOVE A PERSON

*I*f you are trying to remove someone away from you, you can:

1. Get their footracks, their photo, or any personal items
2. Burn them to ash
3. Mix them with a little dirt from each corner of the crossroads and add:
   Sulfur
   Red Ants
   Red Pepper
4. Close the ingredients in a jar until the ants die
5. Then starting at the road outside your home going AWAY from your home sprinkle the ash while petitioning God to remove this person from your life

The ants will go crazy trying to get out of the jar; the target will do the same thing trying to get away from you.

This trick may seem like Hot Foot but it's not because you are adding the person's personal items to this powder. Their items link the person to the work. It is definitely not the same as Hot Foot!!! When you use Hot Foot powder it can reach out and touch ANYONE that gets in it. When you make this powder and lock it down in a jar until the ants are dead using personal items you're doing two things: (1) a jar Conjure and (2) removing them from your home when you start sprinkling on the road going AWAY from your house.

CROSSROADS PROTECTION

The crossroads is also good to work with for cleansing and protection work. An old work you can do to keep tricks from being thrown at you is to go to a 4 way crossroads or intersection.

1. Gather dirt from each corner
2. Pay three pennies at each corner
3. In the middle of the crossroads pour a shot glass of Whiskey
4. When you get home put a small pile of crossroads dirt in all 4 corners of every room in your home with a pinch of Salt and Sulfur on top of the dirt
5. Once a month sweep your corners from top to bottom and gather the dirt you laid at each corner
6. Bring this dirt to the crossroads and leave it there
7. Repeat the process

This old trick will protect you and your house from being attacked. It also keeps away haints.

CROSSROADS MONEY DRAW

You can work with the crossroads to DRAW you MONEY and LOCK it down!

To start the work:

1. Go to your local bank and get a $5
2. When you bring the $5 bill home go somewhere private and take off all your clothes
3. Rub the $5 bill UP your body from your FEET to the top of your HEAD

It is important that the money touch your skin because you are drawing it to you!

4. Then gather dirt from the four corners of the crossroads
5. Add the dirt to a medicine bottle
6. Fold the $5 bill towards you with the face looking out
7. To the medicine bottle add:

   Bayberry
   Solomon's Seal
   A piece of licorice root
   Frankincense
   Pyrite
   A magnet (cause we want to make a BIG DRAW!)

8. Close your bottle up and burn a tealight on top of the bottle
9. Call on the crossroads spirit to draw money into your home

Do this for three days.

10. On the fourth day take the bottle and leave it at the crossroads overnight.
11. Tell the crossroads spirit that you are leaving the bottle there for him to empower so you'll always have prosperity in your home.

12. The next day, go to the crossroads and get your bottle and keep it in a safe place in your home or you can put it by your front door. I keep my money bottle by my front door.
13. Once a month burn a three day tealight on the bottle and take it to the crossroads overnight to be refreshed.

Remember to shake your bottle when you're calling on the spirit and thank him for blessing you with money.

To Bring a Lover to You

1. Get a Medicine Bottle
2. You need dirt from the person's home
3. Personal items
4. Burn the personal items to ash and mix it with the dirt add:
   Loveage
   Jezebel Root
   Pyrite
   Lodestone
5. Go the crossroads and get a pinch of dirt from each corner.
6. Add this to your medicine bottle.
7. Once you have the bottle together call the spirit of the crossroads into the bottle.
8. With your medicine bottle go the person's house and starting at the front of their house sprinkle a pinch of dirt all the way up to your doorway.

Make sure you leave some of the work in your bottle.

9. Burn tealights around the bottle in the form of the cross
10. Continue working the bottle
11. Once you get results if you want you can bury the medicine bottle in your yard as long as it is not buried in the West

Bottles and Containers

Blue Bottles and Medicine Bottles

Old Conjure workers have always worked with cobalt blue bottles. These special bottles are good for protection, locking things down, healing, and hiding your work. In really old work the old-timey Conjure doctors would treat their bottles with special roots and ingredients then hang them on trees for strong protection. If you walk into an old worker's home and look behind the door nine times out of ten you'll find a loaded blue bottle there. You can do any work with a blue but protection is most common. In line after the blue bottle is the medicine bottle. This can be any type of bottle that has held medicine. I'm not sure why these little bottles are so powerful but they are. You don't hear much about them in this new age of internet Hoodoo. I attribute this to there being very few traditional Conjure workers on the internet. Below are a few works that can be placed in either type of bottle.

To Hide something From Your Enemies:

1. Write your secret on a petition paper
2. Put it in the bottle with:
   Slippery Elm
   Red Pepper
   A pinch of Red Pepper
   Poppy Seed
   Grains of Paradise
3. Fill the bottle with Whiskey

4. Seal it
5. Put it in a triangle setup of tealight candles
6. Pray to the Trinity that it be hidden from your enemies

TO REVERSE CROSSED CONDITIONS BACK TO YOUR ENEMIES:

1. Write ALL MY ENEMIES on a piece of paper
2. Lock your enemies in a circle and cross
3. Then cleanse yourself with a small chain
4. Wrap the chain around the name paper
5. Put it in a blue bottle with:
    A razor blade
    Closed safety pin
    Alum
    Sulfur
    Molasses
    Poppy Seed
    Devil's Shoe-String *(to hobble your enemies.)*
6. Fill bottle with Whiskey and place in a circle candle setup

We're using the circle because it is never ending so the work can't get out.

FOR PROTECTION

You need:
    Angelica Root
    Master of the Woods
    Calamus Root
    Devil's Bit to hobble the devil
    A pinch of Red Pepper to heat the work
    Solomon Seal Root
    Frankincense
    Lightning struck wood

1. Put your name in the bottle and fill with Whiskey
2. Set the bottle on a picture of the Holy Family
3. Light candles around it in the sign of the cross. Light the candles from top to bottom and right to left.

To Protect a Marriage or Relationship:

1. Get a photo of you and your spouse together
2. Write your petition across the photo
3. Sign your names on it with your name over your lovers
4. Dress the four corners with domination oil
5. Burn the photo to ash
6. Put the ash in your bottle with:

   A hair from the crown of your head and your spouse
   Angelica Root for protection
   Master of the Woods
   Loveage root
   Damiana
   Lightning struck wood *(for strength and power in the marriage)*
   Solomon Seal for wisdom in the marriage
   A strong magnet
   A piece of Pyrite

7. Light a blue, purple, and red candle in a line with the bottle in front of the middle candle which is purple

The blue candle protects and soothes your marriage, the purple is for strength and power while the red is for love and honor in your marriage.

Honey Jar Container Conjure

So much of this information is being lost or is being changed by intellectual folks. The thing is they talk a good game so folks tend to believe what they say is true; but for someone who grew up living this work daily we know the difference. It's just a sad thing to see happen to something that you grew up with. Over the years the containers I have used and or been instructed to use by my elders include, Coffee cans {not just any ole can but a can that has held coffee}, copper pot or bowl, {copper draws prosperity} or an iron pot. I have an ole iron pot that MiMi gave me many years ago. When I am trying to nail someone or something down the work is started in that iron pot. Iron is powerful because it is almost unbendable also iron comes from deep in the earth and has its own natural power. In the ole days folks used cans instead of iron pots because the iron pots were used for cooking and washing. The coffee can is the next best thing and they work really well. I think it is the power of the coffee that was stored in the can that makes them work so well. Tin is good for works but it is not as strong as iron. It bends and is wonderful for works that are of the "bend over nature". Copper represents wealth, its shiny and copper draws so any copper bowl or pot would be good for prosperity work. My money pot is an ole copper bowl. From what I have learned pot, bowl, or can all work the same if you are trying to do a container work.

Money Can

Everyone needs a steady flow of cash to live. The thing with money Conjure is you have to keep it going. You can't light a candle and say a few prayers and expect all this money to start flowing in. Money work is an ongoing work. To start your money can you need to:

1. Do a spiritual cleansing
2. Then take a photo of yourself
3. Place the photo in a large tin coffee can
4. On top of your photo place a large magnet
5. Get:
   A bag of seven bean soup mix
   Crossroads Dirt
   Dirt from the four corners of your home
   Some shredded money
   Some change out of your wallet

6. Mix all these together and pour it into the can

7. Keep a candle of your choice burning in your can at all times

8. Burn stick incense right in the money can

9. Say your prayers and petition for God to bless you with a flow of money so you can support yourself and your family

CONTAINER CONJURE

To dominate your man with using a coon bone to work with:

1. You write his name on a piece of paper
2. Then write your name over his and wrap it around
3. You can use a photo too if you have one
4. Braid red ribbon around the coon bone TOWARDS you until the name or photo is completely covered
5. Tie five knots and say your petition with each knot
6. Then tie your coon bone around a purple vigil candle
7. Put the purple vigil in a red bowl and add:
   Daimiana
   Loveage
   Master of the Woods
   Lightning struck wood
   Jezebel Root
8. Cover the bowl with Karo Syrup and Whiskey to feed your work.

Hoodoo Honey Verses Syrup or Sugar

Growing up syrup was all that my mama ever kept around the house, honey cost too much that's what the rich folk had. When I was a young worker I was taught to use syrup in my sweetening work; but now a day's all folks seem to know about is working with honey. I think the reason folks thought honey was good for sweetening is because one it draws, and two it is sweet. Honey works really slow. Anything that pours SLOW is going to work slowly. That's one of the first things I learned as a young worker. Folks who don't have hands on Traditional teacher or wasn't raised in a home where Conjure was part of their daily lives miss all these tidbits of information that is vital to Conjure work. Syrup on the other hand is not only sweet but pours much faster, therefore you get faster results. Sugar also pours fast, sweetens and can be mixed with syrup to make a powerful sweetening jar. You don't have to take my word for it, try it yourself see if the results aren't different.

SHAKE THAT JAR

There seems to be a lot of confusion or misunderstanding about shaking up your work. In the end it doesn't matter who says what it is up to the worker to do what they think is best. People complain to me all the time about their honey jars that don't work; and I always say the same thing "maybe they ain't working cause you are just letting them sit there". Burning a candle on a jar without any movement is a waste of a good candle and it just makes a big ole mess. This information came out of the Hyatt books; folks need to learn to use their common sense. Here's an example that every good cook knows. If you are cooking beans and you don't stir them they will STICK to the bottom of the pot and burn. So if you are doing this honey jar and everyone knows the honey will crystallize over time that is why syrup works best; you put it together then you sit it on a space and leave it there the only thing that is gonna happen for a long time is all the ingredients will go to the bottom of the jar and do NOTHING.

I'm not saying that it is wrong to work this way, I don't have the right to say someone is doing THEIR work wrong; I'm just saying that without movement nothing will happen. When you shake the jar up you are causing the work to shift, to move around. That along with your prayer and petition will get the jar moving. Another thing I have never gotten is why is it so important to have the candle melt all over the jar. This just makes a big mess. Maybe the idea of letting the candle melt all over the jar was to cover the jar. I guess it is all in what we are taught; but if you ask ten people how their honey jars work at least seven will say they work slowly.

DOMINATION JAR

For this jar Conjure you need to get:

A baby food jar
Photo
Syrup
Magnet
Jezebel Root
Calamus
Dirt Daubers Nest
Master of the Woods
Rosemary

1. Place your entire ingredient into the jar and cover them with syrup
2. Close the lid tightly on the jar
3. Shake the jar really hard three times each time demanding what you want

I have seen this jar work within hours of making it. I have made this jar on my own husband. Once we weren't speaking to each other unless the children were around. Well I got tired of it and made the jar. He was at work and before the hour was out he called me and acted like nothing had happen. Sometimes you have to hammer them when they are being bull headed.

SWEETENING JAR

This jar is good when you need to sweeten a boss for a friend. You need:

A baby food jar
Some Lavender to smooth
Dirt Daubers Nest
Master of the Woods
A photo if you have it or something personal
A magnet

1. Add all the ingredients into the jar and cover it with powder Sugar
2. Burn a tea light on the jar daily
3. Call on your targets spirit and demand they be sweet towards you

You will see a big difference in the way they act towards you.

DRY MONEY JAR

Sugar
Magnet
Five Finger Grass
Blue Flag
Some change
Hair from the crown of your head

Genesis 22v14

"And Abraham called the name of that place Jehovahjireh: as it is said to this day, In the mount of the LORD it shall be seen."

SHUT YOUR MOUTH JAR

Get a photo of the target
Place it in a small baby food jar

1. Load the jar with:
Red Pepper
Gunpowder
Dill to sour them
A needle and thread to sow their mouth shut
Cover the ingredients with milk

Use milk because not only does it coat the tongue when you drink it but it also sours.

2. Burn a tea light on the jar daily

3. Then shake the jar to stir the target up

I have made this jar and it seems to keep on working as long as you leave the jar together.

SOURING JARS

What does a souring jar do? To be blunt; a souring jar is made to SOUR someone's life! You don't get to pick and choose what part of their life you are souring; the jar sours their whole life until it is busted period! There is a misconception with workers who have learned on-line Hoodoo about these jars. Real time Conjure workers would have been taught better. This just proves what I have said all along, internet Hoodoo's only learned part of the work.

If you place a couple in a souring jar to separate them then you are SOURING BOTH PEOPLE! Why would anyone do that?

Maybe because they don't know any better! The only person that is put in the jar is the TARGET! Folks need to understand that when you sour a relationship that persons whole life is soured; money, love, job, family every aspect of the targets life. Folks really need to stop messing around with this work if they don't know what they are doing.

Common sense will tell you anyone placed in a souring jar will be soured; that is a fact! So why am I hearing about so called workers doing these jars and crossing folks up? They are not only putting the target in the jar but the other person in the relationship in the jar; therefore they are both being soured. Some of these folks are claiming it has been handed down in their families; well I don't want them doing work for me. Folks are taking Conjure much too lightly when it can in fact be dangerous and you can ruin someone's life if you don't know what you are doing. This is not a game or an easy way to make money you are dealing with real folks who depend on your knowing what you claim to know.

MIRROR BOXES

Since this section is about is about bottles and container I'm going to add "mirror boxes" to this section. Like honey jars some folks are under the impression that "mirror boxes" can and are only used to hold an enemy down. They are also under the misconception that mirrors are on used for this type of work. These same folks don't think that mirrors are used any other way in traditional Conjure; they seem to think it is a mixture of Conjure and a Mexican folk magic. This tells me two things; one these folks have never been to the Deep South, and two they ALL learned from the same person. If you travel into the Deep South you will see mirrors in the windows of some of the homes. I was raised in such a home where mirrors were placed in the windows facing the road. This is passed down four generations in my family; my own children being the fourth.

The mirrors that are kept in the windows are there to deflect any roots or ill wishes being thrown at the house. If you shine a light into a mirror you will see what I mean; the light will jump off the mirror and come back to its source. Fact always wins over fiction. The fact is that a mirror box with the mirrors facing outward will deflect anything sent to that box. With that in mind if you work a protection box and put yourself in the box anything that is thrown at you will be sent back. That's a fact not fiction. That is also conjuring at its best. When folks are so firm in pointing out a work is wrong it makes me wonder why? To every positive there is a negative, black to white, light to dark, why would anyone think that mirrors can't be worked with in Conjure to defend or cross. Another fact is that deep southern Conjure workers do work with mirrors. I don't understand how folks who have never met a true Conjure worker can make such positive blatant statements as fact. All these statements I feel comes from one source "the Hyatt books".

Protection Mirror Box

If you find yourself in need of a protection mirror box the first step is to do a spiritual cleansing. This is very important because you don't want to place yourself in a mirror box if you are crossed up or have other issues going on. I would take at least one spiritual bath using:

> A strong cup of black coffee
> Four table spoons of table Salt
> One cap of Lemon Juice
> Pray *Isaiah 41* either before, during or after your bath

Once you have taken the bath you need to take a photo of yourself. You need:

1. Two slices of Angelica Root.
2. Place your photo between the roots
3. Make a packet using red cotton thread.
4. Petition whatever spirit you like to protect you.
5. Lay a bed of bay leaves in the box and place your packet on them.
6. Place an opened safety pin on top of the packet
7. Then cover it with another layer of bay leaves.
8. Close your box
9. Make a set up of five tea lights, four in the crossroads set up and one to burn on top of the box.
10. Petition your higher power to protect you against those who would wish you ill.

Mirror Box

Now this box is a little different from the protection box. This box is used to hold an enemy down. This is the mirror box everyone knows how to make. I'm going to give you a very basic recipe. You need:

> A small box that has been painted black
> Broken glass

Sulfur
Crossroads dirt
Graveyard dirt
Spider webs
Black Mustard Seeds
Something of the targets

1. Combine all the ingredients and make a bed of the in the box
2. Place the target in the box
3. Using a square head nail; nail them down
4. Then cover them with the rest of the ingredients
5. Close the lid and nail it shut

After that it is up to you how far you will go with this box

Protection Mirror

1. Using a photo of yourself
2. Write the word protection over your head
3. Get a 7 day white candle and cleanse it with Holy Water
4. Write your name and the word protection in the wax
5. Then put a bit of protection oil on your finger and going clockwise dress the candle
6. Then mix:

    Salt

    Angelica

    Rue

7. Once you have everything together take your photo and place it UNDER the mirror face up
8. Then place your candle in the center of the mirror
9. Next sprinkle your herbal mixture around the candle
10. Say 3 our Fathers and light the candle
11. Then call on Saint Michael and ask him to guard you and keep you safe and to defeat those who would cause you harm

Repeat this daily until the candle burns out.

12. Then take your photo from under the mirror and fold it towards you until it is small
13. Get you a red piece of flannel
14. Then place the photo and the herbal mixture from the mirror and sew it up

Carry this on you. You now have a protection hand. Feed it protection oil once a week on the day you started the work on.

Protection Work

1. Get you two small mirrors
2. Place your photo after you have done a cleansing between the BACKSIDES of the two mirrors
3. The side you look into will be facing outward
4. Bind the mirrors together with red thread; just enough to hold them together
5. Place the mirror either at the back of your altar where it won't be seen or in a safe place

This packet will deflect anything sent to harm you.

To Block, Bind, and Return

If someone is really causing trouble and nothing you do seems to work; then this will help you. There are some people you just can't be good too. They live on making other people miserable. You know the ole saying misery loves company. They seem to be able to stir up as much crap as they can and they are never to blame. They basically get off free of their actions. People don't see them as they really are. Well this little mirror trick will not only bind them but turn all their ugliness back on them. You need:

A photo of the person
Two small mirrors
Some black thread

1. Place the photo between the two mirrors with the backs of
   the mirrors facing outward
2. Bind the mirrors with the black thread

They will be trapped inside of the mirrors and everything they do will be reflected back on them. This may seem very simple but it is a powerful work. No matter which way they turn they will see only themselves. When they have learned their lesson you can release the spell by cutting the thread and by taking the photo from between the two mirrors.

Candles and Lamps

Candles

I wasn't going to add a "candle section" to this workbook because everyone knows how to burn a vigil or do they? In the old days before we had electricity I don't believe workers wasted their candles for Conjure work. They needed the candles to be able to have light in their homes. Back then every candle was a taper and tapers were hand dipped. I don't know how many of you know how to make tapers but let me tell you it is a lot of work. It takes hours of dipping a wick in wax to make a good size taper candle. I think that they used oil lamps in their work. I never saw my mama burn a candle; she used an old oil lamp. I think that was what she started out using. I personally like candles. I'm a Leo and I like the flame of a candle. I could do my work without using vigils but I choose not to, I like them. I like the vibration of the wax in a vigil.

I grew up hearing old workers say *"a black candle will drive away evil but a white one can kill you"*. You don't hear any of the so called *"traditional Conjure workers"* talk about working with a white vigil this way. Wonder why? I'll tell you why because they were never taught to work with a white vigil or candle in this way! There are some old workers who will only use white vigils. I have heard them say that is all they need to get a job done. In this day and time folks limit their work because that is what whoever taught them was taught. Don't get me wrong I love colored vigils and I work with them a lot, but if I don't have the right color I will use white nothing will stop me from doing my job. Conjure was built on using what you have on hand. New workers seem to put limits on what can and can't be used in the work. Don't fall into that trap. New workers can't seem to do a job without a bunch of products to help get the job done. Why, because that is what they were taught. I hope this workbook will change some of that.

I sell products also but I don't push them, I don't tell folks you have to have this and this to get a job done. That would be a lie and I don't lie ever! I'm going to say it again you don't have to have a bunch of stuff to get a job done. Use your common sense folks. I am going to share with you the way I do my candles in my work. I have been burning vigils for almost forty years and have been taught by some of the best. I want to pass some of this knowledge on so it want die out. Let's face the facts folks the old traditional Conjure workers are dying out. With them the work is being lost. I see folks all day long claiming to be traditional workers but once they open their mouth to speak about the work I have a good idea of where they got their information from. Folks tend to be the shadow of the teacher. That teacher right or wrong will always be a part of their work.

I was taught that wax has a memory that is why vigil work is so effective. When I buy vigils the first thing I do when I get them home is wipe them down with a wash made of ammonia and Salt. That strips away anything the vigil might have picked up in the store. I then bless them in the three highest names once this is done I put them up until I need them. It depends on the job I am doing as to how I fix my vigil. I do different things for different jobs. For the sake of space in this section I am going to tell you about three ways I was taught to work a vigil. I was taught that if you are bringing something to you, the first thing you do is hold the vigil out at arm's length and roll it too you three times; while stating your petition. If you are removing something then you roll it away from you three times. Again do this while you are stating your petition. By doing this you have already set into motion how the work will flow. The vigil now knows that its job is to either bring something to you or to remove something. I was taught that in order to have success you have to do more than one thing to make a job successful.

If I need to do an uncrossing or a reversal vigil, I roll the vigil away from me three times. Then I wipe myself down with the vigil starting at the crown of my head I wipe myself going downward to the bottom of my feet. I make at least five passes over my body while praying. Once the vigil feels heavy I will light it. I don't dress or feed my reversal or uncrossing vigils. I was taught to let whatever they were taking off of me feed them. If they are already full when you wipe yourself off with them then they won't draw off of you what is there. This is an old Conjure concept that new workers don't know about or it would be all over the internet or in books written about Conjure. When I feel like the vigil has done its job before I light the vigil I speak my petition into the vigil. Then I light the vigil. This is also something that is not talked about so this tells me that not too many people know about this. If I feel like the one vigil isn't going to be enough to remove whatever is there then I will repeat the process and light another vigil right before the first one goes out. This is an effective way to remove blocks and to help get relief from a crossed condition.

When I need to bring in a little extra money I will burn a money drawing vigil. I roll the vigil to me, and then I use a nail to write in the wax. I write my name first going in a circle around the vigil. Then next to the wick I write "the Lord is my shepherd I shall not want" It doesn't matter if the words over lap or if you can't read it just write it as close to the wick as you can. Then I take a screw driver and I make four holes in the wax; top, bottom, right and then left. This will make the sign of the crossroads. I then load my vigil. I place a little oil and powders in my vigil, because if you over load them then they will catch on fire.

I tape a photo of myself on the outside of the vigil looking in. That way my spirit watches the flame burning as the vigil burns. The last thing I do before I light my vigil is hold it up close to my mouth and pray my petition into the wax. Then I light my vigil.

ATTRACTION CANDLE WORK

Here is a simple but effective attraction work. Remember Conjure is all about working with what you have on hand.

1. Dress your red candle with oil that you have prayed *Song of Solomon 3 V 1-4* into
2. Using a nail (to nail them down) write the targets name in the wax
3. Tape a photo of the target which you have written 3V 1-4 across the photo to the candle
4. Fix the photo where the target will be looking at the flame of the candle as it burns
5. Set your candle in a bowl that you have placed a flat sheet of magnet in
6. Pour syrup around your candle
7. Then light the candle
8. Pray 3 V 1-4 over the candle 3 times daily, while calling the targets name out after each verse

   1 By night on my bed I sought him whom my soul loveth: I sought him, but I found him not.

2 I will rise now, and go about the city in the streets, and in the broad ways I will seek him whom my soul loveth: I sought him, but I found him not.

3 The watchmen that go about the city found me: to whom I said, Saw ye him whom my soul loveth?

4 It was but a little that I passed from them, but I found him whom my soul loveth: I held him, and would not let him go, until I had brought him into my mother's house, and into the chamber of her that conceived me.

COME TO ME CANDLE

You need:

A bowl

A photo of the target

A flat magnet to set in the bowl

Loveage

Master Root

Calamus

Pomegranate juice

Powdered Sugar

1. Tear out *Songs of Solomon 4 V1-8* out of your Bible and write your target's name on it
2. Fold it to you and bind it up with the red string
3. Place the packet into the bowl
4. Set an orange candle over the packet
5. Sprinkle all the dry ingredients around the candle
6. Then pour the Pomegranate juice into the bowl
7. Light your candle
8. Pray your petition over the candle three times

Repeat this daily until you see the results you are looking for.

1 Behold, thou art fair, my love; behold, thou art fair; thou hast doves' eyes within thy locks: thy hair is as a flock of goats, that appear from mount Gilead.

2 Thy teeth are like a flock of sheep that are even shorn, which came up from the washing; whereof every one bear twins, and none is barren among them.

3 Thy lips are like a thread of scarlet, and thy speech is comely: thy temples are like a piece of a Pomegranate within thy locks.

4 Thy neck is like the tower of David builded for an armoury, whereon there hang a thousand bucklers, all shields of mighty men.

5 Thy two breasts are like two young roes that are twins, which feed among the lilies.

6 Until the day break, and the shadows flee away, I will get me to the mountain of Myrrh, and to the hill of frank- incense.

7 Thou art all fair, my love; there is no spot in thee.

8 Come with me from Lebanon, my spouse, with me from Lebanon: look from the top of Amana, from the top of Shenir and Hermon, from the lions' dens, from the mountains of the leopards.

LAMPS

I personally like working with candles. I like the way the wax holds the petition and the prayers that are said into the vigil. I also like working with oil lamps you don't really have to worry about them catching on fire and you can set the flame at a low steady burn. You can fill the base with herbs, roots, personal items of the target and anything else you want to add to the work.

Oil lamps are wonderful for ongoing jobs and they cost less than keeping candles going. In the ole days the lamps had to be filled with kerosene that is the fuel that was used back then. You could smell it the minute you walked in the door. Today you can find a lamp oil at any craft store called "liquid candle oil" it has absolutely no smell and doesn't smoke unless you have the wick turned up too high. There is another plus when using an oil lamp; it want catch on fire if you over load the base. That is one of the things I don't like about candles; if you overload them they either go out or they catch on fire. A candle also puts out more heat than an oil lamp does, so this is another plus for using the lamps.

When my Dad passed and we were cleaning out the storage room I found one of my mama's ole lamps. I brought it home so I could use it. When I took it apart to clean it I found something I had never seen before. There was a strip of baby blanket pinned to the wick. There had been writing on it but I couldn't make it out. There was also dried stuff in the bottom of the bowl; it took me days to clean it out. I think the lamp may have been used for healing work because that is the feel it had. I'm not sure but I learned something new from my mama even though she is gone. If you pin your petition to end of the wick in your oil lamp it seems to make the work stronger. I think it is because the flame is on one end and the petition is on the other end. This is how I work my lamps now.

Once you find the lamp you will use in your work you need to cleanse the lamp before you use it. Wipe the lamp down with a mixture of 1 cap of ammonia to about 16 oz of water. Make sure you pour some of the mixture in the bowl of the lamp. Rinse the lamp well with cool running water; then set the lamp a side to dry. When the lamp is dry dress the lamp with some type of spiritual oil; make sure you dress the inside of the lamp too. Hold the lamp up to your mouth and pray *Psalm 23* into the lamp. Now your lamp is ready to use.

MARRIAGE LAMP

This lamp can be worked to keep a marriage safe from interference and to keep the love alive. You need a lamp that has been cleansed. You need:

Loveage
Jezebel Root
Dixie John Root
Angelica Root
Devils Shoestring
Solomon Seal Root
2 magnets

I want to explain why I used these ingredients.

Loveage does a few things, it draws love but it also heals and promotes self love. It helps you feel loved so it is an herb to add to any type of love work or self improvement work.

Jezebel Root promotes woman's power and helps women stay in control.

Dixie John does a few things it moves obstacles out of the way and draws in blessings. Some folks might not agree with this but this is what I have experienced using the root.

Angelica Root is a holy root so I added it for blessings.

Devils Shoestring is added to hobble the devil so nothing can interfere.

Solomon Seal Root is added for wisdom and the power of Solomon.

1. Lay your roots and herbs out on a white handkerchief.
2. Set four tea lights around them in the cross set up,
3. Light the tea lights and pray your petition over them.
4. Take the Song of Solomon 4 out of the Bible and write your petition over it.

5. Place the petition into the lamp then add your roots and herbs.
6. Take a photo of you and your spouse.
7. Place the photo's so you are face to face
8. Then place a magnet on each side to hold the photo's together.
9. Place the packet into the lamp.
10. Hold the lamp up to your mouth and pray into it:

"*The Lord is my Sheppard I shall not want*".

Pray it three times into the lamp.

11. Fill the lamp with oil and light it.
12. Turn the flame down low.

Go at least once a day and pray your petition over your lamp. When the oil gets low just refill the lamp.

HEALING LAMP

This healing lamp can be worked by its self or be worked along with hands on healing. You need:

Rue Angelica
Lemon Grass
Devil's Bit
Master of the Woods
Devils Shoestring

1. Take a photo of the person who is ill
2. Set the photo on top of a white handkerchief
3. Cover the photo with the roots and herbs
4. Place a cross set up around the roots and herbs
5. Place one tea light in the center of them
6. Pray Hosea 6 V1-4 over the ingredients
7. After each verse call out the person's name that is to be healed
8. Pray over the set up at least three times before the tea lights go out

9. When the tea lights going out add all your ingredients into your lamp
10. Hold the lamp up to your mouth and pray the Hosea and your petition into the lamp
11. Fill the lamp with lamp oil and light it

You need to go three times a day when the hands are going downward on the clock and pray *Hosea 6 V1-4* and your petition for healing. Remember to call the person's name out after each verse is prayed.

> *1 Come, let us return to the LORD; for it is he who has torn, and he will heal us; he has struck down, and he will bind us up.*
> *2 After two days he will revive us; on the third day he will raise us up, that we may live before him.*
> *3 Let us know, let us press on to know the LORD; his appearing is as sure as the dawn; he will come to us like the showers, like the spring rains that water the earth.*
> *4 What shall I do with you, O Ephraim? What shall I do with you, O Judah? Your love is like a morning cloud, like the dew that goes away early.*

PROTECTION LAMP

Let's face it not everyone is gonna like us in this life. When someone doesn't like you it is only human nature that they wish ill will towards you. I think folks are under the misconception about just how powerful hatred can be. Folks don't have to be a worker to cause you harm. If they dislike you enough and think about you enough that is just as harmful as if someone Conjured you. It is always good to keep your protection up. For this lamp you need:

A set of small mirrors
A photo of yourself or your family.

1. Place the photo in the center of the two mirrors with mirror side facing outward on both sides

2. Using red cotton thread bind the mirror packet together
3. Set the packet on a white hankie
4. Lay on top of the packet:
   Angelica Root
   Master of the Woods
   Calamus
5. Make a cross set up with tea lights
6. Pray your petition over the set up along with *Deuteronomy 33 V 27-29*

Pray over the set up when the hands of the click are moving upward because you are drawing the protection of God around you.

7. Say your petition and prayer at least three times before the tea lights go out
8. When the tea lights go out place all the ingredients in the lamp
9. Hold the lamp up to your mouth and pray your petition and *Deuteronomy 33 V 27-29* into the lamp
10. Fill the lamp and light it; keep the lamp going with a low flame near the front door of the house

Say your prayer and petition daily over the lamp as the hands of the clock are moving upward.

27 He subdues the ancient gods, shatters the forces of old; he drove out the enemy before you, and said, 'Destroy!'

28 So Israel lives in safety, untroubled is Jacob's abode in a land of grain and wine, where the heavens drop down dew.

29 Happy are you, O Israel! Who is like you, a people saved by the LORD the shield of your help, and the sword of your triumph! Your enemies shall come fawning to you, and you shall tread on their backs.

PROSPERITY LAMP

We all need a little prosperity in our lives. When you are working on prosperity you have to do more than one thing. Just setting a light or making a sweetening jar is not enough; in order to bring in true prosperity. You have to keep the flow of work going. In this section you will see how to set up you money lamp, in some of the other sections you will find more helpful ways to draw in prosperity. The combination of these things will help draw to you the success you are looking for. Keeping the home fire going success and prosperity can be yours.

1. Get your lamp and follow the regular instruction for cleansing the lamp.
2. Lay out your white handkerchief and place on the hankie:
   A magnet
   Pyrite
   Dixie John Root
   Five Finger Grass,
   Bayberry
   Master of the Woods
   Some money from your wallet
3. Fix your tea light set up and pray Deuteronomy 8 V 13-18 over your ingredients.
4. Pray while the hand of the clock is moving upward to draw prosperity into your home.
5. Pray over the set up three times while the tea lights are burning.
6. When the tea lights burn out place all your ingredients into the bowl of your lamp.
7. Hold the lamp up to your mouth and pray your chapter and verses into the bowl.
8. Fill the bowl with oil and place the lamp on your prosperity altar.

Pray over it daily.

CHALK

USING CHALK IN CONJURE

I was taught as a young worker to use white chalk to mark my doors, my windows, and any work I needed to mark; you don't hear about the use of chalk in Conjure work in this day and age. Today most workers use what is called cascarilla, which is nothing more than powdered eggshells. Cascarilla is used in VooDoo, Santeria, Palo and other religions to mark things with. Although new folks coming into Conjure use Cascarilla it is not part of Conjure. When folks have never been taught something they incorporate things into the work that they do know about; because of this the use of chalk in traditional Conjure work is dying out and being replaced with something else that is not Hoodoo. I don't mean any disrespect

to anyone I am just stating the facts. It's possible that cascarilla is used in New Orleans style hoodoo but it is not used in Traditional Southern Style Conjure. I am a very traditional Conjure worker, I don't like all these changes that I see being made. Again I mean no disrespect to anybody, but if you went to Georgia, Mississippi, or South Carolina, and asked old folks there what cascarilla was they wouldn't have a clue what you were talking about; unless they were on-line and read it somewhere; which I doubt.

Every time someone removes something from the old way root workers have worked for many years they are changing Conjure. Whether they mean to do this or not it is being done. I think a lot of this has to do with not having the knowledge or I should say not having all the knowledge of some of the old works. It is human nature to want to change what we don't understand; Humans always want change things to suit their needs. I think that the use of chalk in Conjure is being lost because folks don't know about it or what to do with it; so it is now being replaced with cascarilla. I was told a couple months ago that I'm forgetting all old works that I know; I plan to rectify that now. I will be adding a lot of old simple but powerful Conjure tricks that I was taught as a young girl. I would love to see that use of chalk brought back into Conjure and use like it was in the old days. There is nothing wrong with cascarilla but that is not traditional to Conjure work, the use of cascarilla belongs to other systems.

Try working with chalk yourself; it makes the work have a whole different feel than cascarilla does. You can get a box of white chalk for a little bit of nothing at the dollar store. All you have to do is:

1. Take that chalk out-of-the-box
2. Pray *Psalm 23* over them
3. Then set you up three white vigils in the shape of a triangle and place your chalk in the center of the set up
4. Go daily to your altar and repeat *Psalm 23* over them until your vigils burn out
5. Once your vigils burn out your chalk is ready to use in your work

You can use this chalk for many things, from bringing blessings to crossing someone up. This is a tool that is very useful and very powerful in Conjure. I don't want to see its use lost.

You can even offer it to your spirits, give it to them to empower and use it when you work with them. La Madama loves chalk; I use it to mark her work with. You can mark the backs of mirrors in your work, boxes, altars, window seals; the list could go on and on to the ways chalk can be used in Conjure work. You can even all a little to your powders and other items you make. You can mark your Mojo hands and your packets with it before you put them together. You can mark your sidewalk and the stoop leading up to your business or home. There are many uses for it in Conjure work only you can set a limit on your work. If you want to work traditional Conjure work then add chalk to your work.

MOJO AND PACKETS

CONJURE BAGS

Traditional Conjure bags are made out of Red Flannel. Basically Conjure bags hold work, so in part they are like a container work. I have heard of folks making these bags out of all kind of materials and different colored cloth; that is not a traditional Conjure bag. Sometimes the bags are placed with a leather bag and worn around the neck. The leather protects the bag and I feel it adds to the power of the bag because the leather came from a living being. You can buy ready-made Conjure bags but the best bag is one you make yourself. You need to pray your petition through the whole process of making the bag. With every stitch you make your petition should be said. Think of this as building blocks towards the finished product.

Once you have your Conjure bag made you need to set it in a candle set up of five tealights. Place your tealights, top, bottom, right, to left. The fifth tealight should be placed on top of the Conjure bag. You should keep this set up going for at least seven days. During the seven days you should pray your petition over your Conjure bag daily. Below you will find a few recipes to get you started.

Conjure Bag Recipes

Law Stay Away

Dirt from a police station,
High John,
Devil's Shoe String,
A pinch of Slippery Elm
Dirt from your front door stoop

Uncrossing Bag

Hyssop
Rue
Sage
A Pinch of Coffee

Love Drawing Bag

Loveage
A magnet
Orange Peel
Calamus
Dirt Daubers Nest

Money Drawing Bag

Money
Five Finger Grass
A Magnet
Nutmeg
Fenugreek Seeds

Conjure Packets

Packets are an old timey Conjure work that you don't hear much about anymore. Everybody knows about the Mojo bag but that is not the same as a packet. Traditional Conjure workers don't limit themselves to just Mojo bags or what I call Conjure hands because there's more than one way to do a job.

A packet is completely different from a Mojo hand because you have to work with it daily. If you make a money packet to draw money to you then you must take it out daily hold it in your hand and pray over it. Most workers feed a Mojo hand and talk to it only once a month but with a packet you have to keep it going every day. If you got a hard case then you have to feed your packet everyday just as you talk to it and tell it to draw exactly what you want.

With a packet you can light vigils on it or tie it around other works you are doing. If you call on a certain spirit like St. Martha for instance then you give the packet to her and petition her to draw exactly what it is you want. Everyday just like you'd feed that packet you'll go to St. Martha and call on her to take care of the job since the packet you made for the situation belongs to her. Packets are wrapped in Red Flannel and tie with Red Cotton String. Nowadays you'll find a lot of new workers who weren't taught traditionally to use red when making a packet. The same applies when making a Mojo bag. Don't use all these different colors.

If you want to DRAW something to you always remember to fold your packet towards you when making it. When you tie the packet you have to also wrap the string TOWARDS you while saying your petition. When removing someone then you fold, wrap, and tie the packet going AWAY from you. When done with your packet tie nine knots and feed a mixture of Whiskey and Conjure Oil. Carry your packet everywhere you go and don't forget to talk to it every day. Hold it up to your mouth and breathe your petition on the packet.

Now I'll give you an example of how to make a packet to DRAW money.

1. Write your petition on a $1 bill
2. Place

   Devil's Shoestring

   Pyrite

   Solomon Seal

   A pinch of Clove on the back of the $1 bill
3. Fold the bill towards you on all sides into a small packet with the face of the bill looking out
4. Then wrap Red Flannel around the packet towards you while calling money to you
5. Repeat the process with Red Cotton String and tie nine knots
6. Feed your little money packet a few drops of Pay Me Conjure Oil.

PRAYER CLOTHS AND STRING IN CONJURE WORK

Working with Prayer Cloths and string is really old and one of the most important items you'll find in Conjure. Prayer cloths are made from a white handkerchief that you have prayed over for 9 days while Red Cotton String is most commonly preferred for most Conjure works. These items are so important because you'll find them in just about any work you hear about in Conjure whether that means making a Conjure hand, putting together a packet, fixing a gris-gris or even preparing a Conjure jar. Most of these works require a prayer cloth to contain your work and red string to bind your work. If you think about it all a Mojo hand is, is a prayer cloth that holds your prayer while the Red Cotton String keeps the power there. The same goes for a packet. So when you think about it the prayer cloth and the string is like the "skin" of your work. It's the largest and most important part of your work because it protects the work you contain and keeps the power there working for you.

Well what a lot don't know is that there are many other uses for the cloth and string in your work. For example if you want to draw something to you write your petition on a square piece of parchment paper. Fold the paper towards you into packet. Place it on your prayer cloth. Fold your cloth towards you into a tube and tie it around your vigil candle. If you want to keep your woman at home write your petition on a large piece of parchment. Place her underwear flat on the parchment and fold your petition around the underwear TOWARDS you into a packet. Then fold your prayer cloth around the bundle TOWARDS you into a tube and tie it around the bottom of your bed post. You can also tie this work around a red and pink vigil named after you and your wife to keep y'all together.

To nail your enemy down write their name on parchment in a circle. Draw a cross over their name in the circle and fold the petition AWAY from you into a packet. Place the paper packet on your prayer cloth and roll away from you into a tube. Wrap and tie the prayer cloth around the sword of St. Michael. Tie the sword facing downward around a red vigil candle that has been dressed with Run Devil Run oil. Before you light the candle pierce the blade of sword facing downward with a photo of your enemy. Make sure the blade stabs your enemy from head to foot. Call on St. Michael to hold your enemies down like he did the demon and keep them there until they leave you alone. Light your candle before on a prayer card of St. Michael.

CONJURE PROTECTION PACKET

Here is a recipe for a *"Packet"* that will protect you from being Conjured.

> Saltpeter — 1 pinch
> Angelica — 1 pinch
> Master of the Woods — 3 pinches
> Salt — 1 pinch
> Sugar — 1 pinch
> The heads of 3 wooden matches

1. As you add a pinch of each say
   "In the name of God the Father, Name of God the Son, Name of God the Holy Ghost"

FIXING A GATOR CLAW

The best use for an Alligator Claw is in a Money Drawing packet.

1. You need to soak the claw in a Whiskey herbal mix so it will become soft.
2. Once it is soft bottle up your Whiskey and use the Whiskey to feed your packet with.

3. You can add:

    Bayberry (for Money)

    Five Finger Grass *(to grab the money)*

    Solomon Seal Root *(to have the wisdom to deal with money the right way)*

    Master of the Woods *(to draw and to make you your own master over your money)*

    A large magnet *(to pull it in)*

It can take a while for the claw to soften but it's ok because you have already got the work started.

4. Place a Mercury dime in the center of the claw and close the fingers around the dime
5. Use red cotton thread to hold the fingers down; once this is done you can start wrapping the hand with red thread
6. Tie the packet off with three knots
7. You can burn tea lights right on top of the packet
8. Pray and petition over your packet at least once a week

Ask the spirit of the gator to help grab your money and to hold it.

You can carry it, hang it beside your front door, or place it in your business by the door to draw money. Just remember to feed it!

CONJURE OILS

In the old days before commercial spiritual oils really came on the market the ole folks would use the oils they found in the drug store. Oils such as Olive Oil, sweet oil and castor oil to name a few. Below is a short list of those oils and how they were used.

LARD

Lord my mama's answer to everything was lard, Sulfur and ash mixed. If we got sick she would slather us down with one of her lard concoctions.

CASTOR OIL

I hate this stuff and I never use it; but it had to be added here because it is a Conjure Oil. Beware this stuff is thick and nasty. My Grandma and mama loved this stuff. Every year we had to take a good dose of this. If we were sick we had to take a dose and depending on what was wrong with us mama might mix it with some stuff and rub it on our chest and our feet. Castor oil is really good for hot oil treatments for your hair. This stuff last for years before it goes bad. Castor oil comes from the castor bean, beans grow on the ground so this oil is good for flightiness as my Grandma would say, and it settles you down in plain English. Rub it on the bottom of your feet. It also helps with dry skin and athlete's feet. It is also good for ring worms; I'm not sure why maybe it suffocates them. This will make a fine Conjure Oil; I just can't stand the smell or the feel of it after growing up being treated with this stuff.

This falls right in with talc powder as far as I'm concerned.

Cod Liver Oil

Cod liver oil is good for Arthritis, it help ease the pain and inflammation when you add Red Pepper to it and mesSage it into the painful area. This is an old remedy. They are now saying that the oil when taken will help slow down the damage Arthritis does to the joints of folks who suffer with it.

Sweet Oil

You may be wondering what in the world sweet oil is; well it is very refined Olive Oil. Sweet oil is good for many things. As a child my mama would doctor my ears with it because I loved to swim and stayed with an earache. Sweet oil coats the ear and dries up excess water you may get from swimming. A cap of your own urine poured in your ear will do the same thing. Sweet oil is also good for poultices because it has a healing quality. You can rub it on bruises and cuts as you would any other medicine because it will also help heal. I was taught as a young teen to rub it around my eyes to keep from having wrinkles when I got older. It is also used to feed your Mojo bags and Conjure packets. You can make a fine Conjure Oil with sweet oil.

OLIVE OIL

Of course everyone knows about Olive Oil, but did you know that you can place garlic in Olive Oil and use it to cure an earache? Not much I can tell you about using Olive Oil that you wouldn't already know. To make a Holy oil add, Frankincense, Cinnamon and Calamus to a bottle of Olive Oil and pray *Psalm 23* into the bottle.

The oils above are not the oils used by workers today. Most workers buy their spiritual oils instead of making their own. I think everyone should know how to make a simple Conjure Oil. There are many different carrier oils out on the market today. Some traditional workers only use Olive Oil to make their spiritual oils with. It really depends on your preference. Just throwing a bunch of ingredients together will not make very powerful spiritual oils; basically all you will have is a oil with some roots and herbs in the bottle. You need to pray over your ingredients and the base oil before and after you put it together. Remember prayer builds power.

When I make my oils for Old Style Conjure they are prayed over from start to finish. They are placed in a candle set up for seven days. Once the seven days is up then they are ready to use. I use my own products and I'm not going to sell something I wouldn't use. Some folks think that just because a oil smells so strong it takes your breath away it must be a good oil. The EO is added to cut down on the use of the carrier oil which in turn makes the oil cheaper to make. I don't like strong smelling oil that over rides my perfume. So below are some recipes so you can make your own Conjure Oils. These are simple three ingredient recipes. You can use whatever base oil you want to. Remember the ingredients are a small part of the power of the oil. Your prayer is what will fill the oil with power.

MONEY DRAWING OIL

Pyrite
Lodestone grit
Five Finger Grass

BEND OVER OIL

Master of the Woods
Calamus
Licorice Root

ATTRACTION OIL

Pyrite
Master of the Woods
Orange Peel

LOVE ME OIL

Loveage root
Master of the Woods
Calamus

DOMINATION OIL

Calamus
Dirt Daubers Nest
Jezebel Root

HEALING OIL

Heals All
Frankincense
Angelica Root

RULE YOUR ROOST

Jezebel Root
Rose Mary
Master of the Woods

POWDERS AND DIRT

POWDERS

I have been making my own supplies for a long time. I hardly ever buy a ready-made product such as bath Salts, oils and powders. I prefer to make my own. The reason being I can pray over the ingredients as I am making the product. If you decide to make your own supplies you will need a grinder to grind up your herbs. I use a coffee grinder; you can find them a Wal-Mart. Workers use different base powders to make their powders. I use rice powder as a base for my powders. This is what I prefer to use for my products; there are other powder bases that can be used. There are a few different categories these powders fall under. Talc powder, graveyard dirt, Sugar, Salt, gunpowder and Sulfur, to name a few that fall under mineral powders. Then you have what I call herbal powders; these can consist of powdered herbs, arrowroot, or cornstarch. Zoological powders consist of dried animal parts, cascarilla (powdered egg shell), dried blood, Dirt Daubers Nest and dried seaman, to name a few. It depends on what the purpose is in making the powder too what is use.

I prefer to use rice powder because I have found that it holds a scent nicely and it absorbs EO Oils. It mixes well with powdered herbs. When you wear it you don't feel like your skin is being smothered. I'm going to give you my recipe for my protection powder but first I want to talk about adding oils to your powders. If you try to add your oils to, cascarilla, talc, or corn starch you will have a big lumpy mess. The powder will turn into a paste. You don't have this problem with rice powder; but if you want to use one of the other types for your base powder I have found the best way to add my oils is to add them to the mixture of herbs I am using to make my powder. To do this blend your herbs you will use in the powder then add your oil to the blended herbs. Stir your herbal mixture and let the oils dry on the herbs; then mix your herbs and oil with your powder. This way you don't have a big mess. The herbs will hold the smell of the oil so your powder will smell good.

Sometimes I color my powders and sometimes I don't. A little Lady named MiMi, may God rest her soul taught me how to make powders. She didn't add oils to her powders, the herbs and the prayers she said over them made them work. Every powder she made was made with herbs and either cornstarch or talc powder. She didn't color them either. As I said I do color my powders sometimes, to do this I use a dried colorant, you can find it at stores that sell soap making supplies. When you make a powder to use in your work you need to pray over them as they are being made. This adds power to your powders. I'll explain how I do this. I blend my herbs, and then add my oils. Once this is dried I will mix it with my rice powder base. Once this is done

I have a large copper bowl I use to hold my powders in while they are being blessed. I pour my finished powder into the bowl, then depending on the type of work I am doing I choose a candle that relates to the work. I use glass-enclosed candles for this. I dress my candle; I then pray my petition into the candle; then place the candle in with the powder. I just push the powder out of the center and set the candle in the hole I made for it. Once this is done, I light the candle and pray over the candle and the ingredients. Here is one of the prayers I use along with *Psalm 23*. You can say any prayer over the powder you want too, these are just the ones I use. Remember your powders won't look like those that come from most spiritual shops because most of them sell colored talc powder nothing more. Once you make your own powders you will see what I am talking about.

PROTECTION PRAYER

In the name of God I walk out.
God the Father be with me,
God the Holy Ghost be by my side.
Whoever is stronger than these three may approach my body and my life; yet whoso is not stronger than these three would much better let me be! J.J.J.

I don't time how long I pray, I just pray from my heart that the powder will do the job that it was made to do. Once I light the candle I leave it burning until it burns out. Every day as long as the candle is burning I will go and pray over the powder. When the candle goes out I take my pendulum and hold it over the powder. I say, *"Show me your power"*. If I don't get a good response I will burn another candle and repeat my prayers again. Once the powder is ready I place it in an airtight container and store it until I need it. Below you will find the recipe for one of my protection powders.

Protection Powder

Base Powder
Rue
Angelica
Bay Leaves
Rose Mary
Sage

Below you will find a variety of recipes to make your own Conjure powders. You have the basic instructions on how to make your own personal powders. You can decide what you want to use as a base powder.

In the old days they used talc powder as the base of all spiritual powders that were made. I personally cannot stand talc powder. Growing up my mama dusted the beds weekly and us children every night after our bathes. I feel like it is suffocating me if I try to wear it. So I use rice powder as my base powder for my products and for my own personal use. You can use whatever you want to; I leave that up to you.

Powder Recipes

Road Opening Powder

Dirt from the four corners of a crossroads
Five Finger Grass
Master of the Woods
Pinch of Gunpowder

Attraction Powder

Lodestone Grit
Orange Peel
File Gumbo

Money Drawing Powder

Money burnt to ash
Dirt from a bank
Lodestone grit
Cinnamon Powder

Love Drawing Powder

Lodestone Grit
Queen Elizabeth
Loveage
Master of the Woods

Ancestor Powder

Photo of Ancestor burnt to ash
A pinch of Graveyard dirt
Loveage
Angelica Root

Hot Foot Powder

There are times in our lives when we just have to rid ourselves of a person; the reasons vary from person to person. Hotfoot work is very powerful and serious work. This is not the type of work you do because someone made you mad. Hotfoot if made right will make the target wonder, their spirit will never be able to find peace.

This should always be a last resort. Am I saying it shouldn't be used? No I'm not. If someone has pushed me so far until I decide to hot foot him or her then I don't really care what effect it has on him or her. I want them out of my life. As I've said before we are each responsible for our actions. I don't just hot foot someone who has made me mad or gotten on my nerves; this has always been a last resort for me. But if the need arises, I will use it in a heartbeat. The safest way to work with hot foot is either in a medicine bottle or a jar; this way it only affects the target and not everyone who gets in it.

This is my own personal hot foot powder. To make the powder you will need a large airtight jar. Then you need to find a fire ant bed. You have to be careful when collecting these ants. If they bite you it can make your run fever. The bites burn like fire and they get very hot. Once you get the ants in the jar they will run around and try to get out. When they settle down I shake the jar to make them start moving again. I will do this four or five times before I leave them alone. They are one of the key ingredients in the hot foot powder; and just like they want to get out of the jar so will the target want to get away. I usually collect the ants when the sun is going down; this is just my preference. I have collected them when I need to make the powder for a quick job, no matter what time of day it was.

When the ants stop trying to get out of the jar; I will add all the other ingredients to the jar. I don't measure the ingredients; I have made this powder enough to know what it should look like when I've added enough of each ingredient.

I probably add:

1. About two tablespoons of Sulfur to the jar
2. About a tablespoon of graveyard dirt
3. Dirt Daubers Nest *(a little of this goes a long way)*
4. J add enough Red Pepper to the dirt so you can see the Pepper in the dirt
5. Once this is done J shake the jar well
6. Last J add the Cornstarch
7. Shake the jar well

Now you should have a nice pink powder. Keep the lid on the jar tight to keep the dampness out. I keep the jar put up until I need to use the powder, then I only take out what I need.

GOOFER DUST POWDER

Goofer dust is used for crossing an enemy. Where hot foot is used to move you out and send you away, goofer dust is used to jinx, harm, and can even cause death in some cases. Some of the symptoms of being goofered are sever pain and swelling in the feet and legs; also severe headaches. To make goofer dust you need graveyard dirt.

I take the dirt from the left foot area of the grave. This is the way I was taught to get the dirt. Then again you can ask other workers and they will all have a different way of collecting the dirt to make goofer dust. Like hot foot powder this dust should be used with care. When making this dust you should be very careful. I'm not going to give a recipe to make this powder because it is just too dangerous. To many new workers think there is nothing wrong with using this powder on someone even though it can cause death. I just wanted to touch on it but I won't give instructions on how to make it or use it.

I will say this; the powder is made from vile things and you really shouldn't use it unless the work is justified.

CROSSING POWER

Crossing powder is another powder that is meant to harm. This powder is used to close a target's roads. In the days gone by one way of using this powder was to make an X with the powder then spit in the center of the x while cursing the target. Let's face it folks if you get caught doing this today at someone's home you may find yourself in jail. As my granny always said there is more ways to skin a cat than one. This is how I use the powder to close someone's roads. When I make my powder I add crossroads dirt to it. I place a small amount from the four corners and a little from the center. This in its self makes the X used when laying the trick for the target. To get the dirt from the center just take you a dust pan and a whisk broom and sweep up a bit of the dust from the center of the road. If I can get a little dirt from where the targets live I will add that to the powder; if I can't then I will use a petition paper and other personal items if I have them. These I burn and add the ashes to the powder. That is as much as I'm willing to share; I won't give my recipe for this powder because it is too dangerous. I just wanted to give you a bit of information on the powder.

DIRT IN CONJURE WORK

COLLECTING DIRT

Gathering dirt from different locations to use in your Conjure work is "Traditional Conjure". Now a-days all you hear folks talk about is "graveyard dirt" but many other types of dirt are used in Old Style Conjure. I work a lot with dirt in my work I love it, you can mix it with powders and it changes the power of the powder. Burying things in the yard is also part of the work; but it seems to be a lot of confusion going on about where to bury things. So we will be touching on that too; because this is also dealing with dirt and is a really big part of the work. Below are some examples so you can get an idea of where to gather the dirt and how to use it.

Bank Dirt — Can be used for Money, or to get a loan

Yard Dirt where dogs have been fighting — Used to Cross

Court House Dirt — Can be used for justice work or Court Case work.

Police Station Dirt — Can be used in all justice work, law stay away or it can be used draw the law to a person

Railroad Tracks, Bus Station, or Airport — Can all be used to either send them away or bring them back this type of dirt is good in hotfoot work

A Church — Protection, repair a broken marriage, healings and blessings

A Hospital — Healings

Corners of the Crossroads — Closing some ones roads, hotfoot or opening someone roads

Graveyard — All types of work

A Prosperous Business — Better Business

GRAVEYARD DIRT

Graveyard dirt can be used in many ways. It can be used in protection, love, crossing and domination work just to name a few. I have heard about many ways to use graveyard dirt over the years. Some say there are certain times to go to the graveyard, certain phases of the moon, what days one should collect dirt on, the list goes on and on. I go anytime I need to petition the spirits for help. I'm not going to wait until the full moon or whatever if I have a job that needs to be done. The only rule I do follow and this is my own rule; is that I won't petition help from spirits who are not my kin or who I didn't know in life. It is very dangerous, when dealing with spirits period; but to contact an unknown spirit that you don't have a clue about is just crazy you have to use common sense.

Just because a person has passed on doesn't mean that they have all of a sudden became a good person. Their spirit is the same maybe even stronger now that they have passed. If you are going to work with graveyard dirt then you need to stick with your blood kin or folks who are like kin to you. This way you know who and what type of person you are petitioning for help. I had never heard about working with dead folks that you didn't know until I read about it.

I want to explain how I approach the graveyard when I need to collect dirt or do work. Every worker has his or her own way of doing this. One way is not better than the others. This is my way; you have to decide the right way for you. There are only two things that I stand firm on and I think everyone should do them before and after you go to collect dirt or do work in the graveyard. Number one is that before you go to the graveyard you need to speak to your ancestors and you need to have strong protection in place; and two when you get out of the graveyard you need to clean yourself by wiping your shoes off with ammonia and dressing them with turpentine and the when you return home you need to do a good cleansing.

Let me explain to you why I follow these two rules. Let's face the facts; spirits roam the graveyard that is where they live. Not all of them are happy about passing on. Some of them can be very nasty. Also when you go there you will be building energy with your prayers or whatever you plan to do. Entities are drawn to this energy you are putting out. Why in the world would you go there without protection? Please use your common sense. Maybe nothing attached itself to you, or maybe it did. Why take the chance, cleanse yourself just to be on the safe side. It's better to be safe than sorry.

Once I have my protection bath, I gather whatever I need to bring with me. Then I go to my ancestor altar, I call on God and my ancestors. I ask them to protect me and keep me safe. I explain to them about the work I will be doing. I say my prayers, and then I leave to go to the graveyard. The whole time I am driving to the graveyard I am praying. Not only that I be protected, but also that the work I will do will be a success. When I get to the road that leads to the graveyard I leave an offering, I call to the keeper of the gate and ask permission to enter. By the time I reach the gate I know if I can go in or not. Then at the gate I will leave another offering. I usually leave three pennies. I can't stress enough how important it is to be respectful when you enter the graveyard. You are there to ask for assistance, ask is the key word here.

When I reach the grave the first thing I do is say a prayer for them. Then I will talk to them for a while, even though I will be paying for the work or dirt no one likes to feel used not even the spirits. When I feel the time is right I will tell them what I need help with. At this point it is important that you listen. Why? Well there have been a few times when I was lead to do something different than what I planned on doing. Not only did the work turn out right but also it was very powerful. When

I'm ready to get my dirt I use my pendulum to find out where is the best place to get the dirt from. I always check myself; I have learned over the years that this is a good habit to have. Sometimes I will get dirt from more than one place on the grave. It just depends on what the pendulum says. Once I did some work to drive someone away from my daughter, I had already made a wax Dollie to which I had mixed hotfoot into the Dollie along with personal items and the ashes of my petition. This probably would have been enough but I wanted to make sure the job was done fast. I was going to take the dirt from the heart area of my mama's grave, because she loved my daughter so much. I knew she would take care of the problem. Instead I was lead to take dirt from the left hand and the foot of the grave. So once again the spirit changed the work to be done. The left hand explains itself but it took me a while to figure out the foot thing. I was puzzled about that all the way home. Then like lights coming on I remember my mama telling us many times that the best way to defeat someone is to walk on them before they can walk on you; meaning put them under your foot. If someone is causing you trouble, write their name on a petition and either place it on the floor and stomp on it or wear it in your shoe to walk on them.

Graveyard work should be more than going to the graveyard for spiritual work. If you are going to be enlisting the dead to help you in your work then you need to help take care of the place they live in. Go once a month and clean up around the graveyard. Leave flowers for your loved ones, say prayers for the dead. Don't just go there when you want something. Be respectful and show them that you care about their spirits.

WORKING WITH GRAVEYARD DIRT

I personally don't use graveyard dirt for love works unless it is in separation work. So you want find anything written here on the use of graveyard dirt in love spells. I'm not going to write about something I have not used myself. You will find information for protection, hotfoot, domination, court casework, and a little more information. Anytime you use graveyard dirt you need to be careful. I always put newspaper over my workspace so it is easy to clean up if I drop some. You don't want this dirt spilt in your house, and if you do happen to get it on the floor or counter clean it up then wipe everything down with ammonia. I like to use lemon-scented ammonia. You also need to remember to pray and protect yourself before you start to work with this dirt. I don't ever let this dirt get on my hands. If some does happen to get on me I wash my hands immediately with ammonia and my arms up to my elbows; followed by Holy Water. This dirt is not something to play around with. So use your common sense and work safely. You also need to take a cleansing bath after you finish this type of work. I use a cup of strong coffee, a cap of ammonia and a cap of vinegar. Remember to clean your head also; by this I mean to get your head wet with the wash.

Let's talk about using graveyard dirt as a protection agent. The idea here is to ask the spirits aid in protecting your person or property. To do this you follow the in- structions on getting the dirt from the graveyard. While you are there tell them what the dirt will be used for. Ask them to protect you and your home. Ask them to set up a barrier around your home, so that no one who means you harm will succeed. Then gather your dirt and take it home. Once you get home you are ready to put your protection down you will also need some other things to go along with the dirt. See the list and instructions below.

PROTECTION POWDER

Graveyard dirt
Slippery Elm *(to hide you from your enemies)*
Basil *(for protection)*
Sulphur *(to drive away and protection)*
Dragons Blood resin *(protection)*

Now that you have all your ingredients it's time to put it all together.

1. You can pray over each herb separate or mix them together then pray over them

I have done this both ways. If you decide to pray over them separate then when you get them mixed you need to pray over the mixture. Just a little warning here about Slippery Elm, it literally hides you so don't get heavy handed with it. Just a pinch will do. When I say my prayers I also call on my spiritual protector and my ancestors, while holding my hands over the ingredients; along with *Psalm 23*, the Lord's prayer and the Creed. I repeat each prayer three times, then I pray my petition over the ingredients; which is that my home and everything in it be protected from anything that is meant to harm it or the people inside.

2. Once the prayers are done I'm ready to go outside and lay down the protection

The protection powder will be placed in holes at the four corners of the property. To do this you need to dig a hole in one corner at a time, sprinkle some powder in the hole while you pray.

3. Then cover the hole up and move on to the next corner

4. Repeat the process until you have all the corners done

5. Now I have a long sidewalk that leads to my front door. I will make a trench on each side of the sidewalk

6. Then going away from my house J sprinkle the power making a turn on the side walk and coming back up to my door

By doing this we are protected coming and going.

7. J will repeat the prayers at least once a month unless J feel like something is going on

There are many more ways to protect your home and self but these will be explained in the protection section.

I know some people live in apartments and don't have yards. Well you can also protect your apartment this way, by making packets of the powder and either placing it on the window seal or you can plant it in a plant. You can also place it in the four corners of your apartment. There are many ways to make it work for you. Don't let not having a yard stop you from protecting yourself and your home.

Burying In the Yard

There seems to be a LOT of confusion about what to bury and where to bury Conjure items in your yard. Again and I know y'all must be tired of me saying this but *"this is where HANDS ON learning is needed"*. This is one of the first and one of the most important things a young Conjure worker should learn. This can be dangerous! You maybe think "Oh how dangerous can this be"? Send me your information and let me bury you in the West and I will show you just how dangerous it can be.

This crap that is being taught on-line about burying came straight out of Hyatt and it is a dangerous crock. I want to explain 'bout the front and back of the house and East to West. I've said this a thousand times and will say it another thousand I'm sure; there is more to Conjure than what folks call "spells". There is a whole concept a whole way of thinking. You have to have the right frame of mind. I'm sorry and I am not dogging anyone but you can't get that out of a book. You have to learn to use your common sense.

Mr. Robert is one of the toughest mentors I have ever had. He is tricky! You see when you are face to face or on the phone you get to interact and ask questions of your teacher it's not the same as e-mail or reading a book or researching Hyatt. In Conjure there is a reason for burying an item in the West or the back of the house. This is done to HOLD SOMETHING OR SOMEONE DOWN OR TO REMOVE SOMETHING. Please get this clear in your mind.

I think the confusion comes in because there is an old work *"my mama did this to my daddy"* where you bury your man's underwear behind the house to keep him home. This nails him down to stop him from rambling.

This again is why it is important to have a teacher so they can explain to you about the whole concept of nailing down and burying in the West/behind the house. Please take this information to heart because you can harm yourself or someone else with this type of work.

EXAMPLES

We now know that whatever is buried in the west or behind is either deployed to hold something or someone down or to remove something or someone.

EXAMPLE 1

The other day I had a client come to me for help. This guy works per job, meaning the work is not a sure thing. He went to a worker who told him to bury his photo behind his house. I guess the concept of the work was to nail down his job. Well that's all good and fine IF he had a steady job. At the time this was done he was OUT of work. He should have never been given this information. It hurt him not helped him; because he then couldn't get work anywhere. This is an inexperienced worker giving advice when they don't know what the hell they are doing. What they did was gave him advice that nailed his broke ass no job self down, so no wonder he couldn't get a job. He could even pay me for the work because he paid the so called worker all the money he had!

This is what SHOULD have happened. He should have been advised to do at least {3} cleansing bathes {just to make sure he was cleansed}. Then some road opening/money drawing work should have been done to draw the work and money to him. ONCE HE WAS WORKING GOOD THEN NAIL HIS ASS DOWN! In doing the work that way, he has jobs coming in, he as money coming in and he is spiritually cleansed. Folks are learning only part of the work; then they try to work for others and end up messing the client up.

When you nail something down it brings everything to a complete STOP, they can't MOVE FORWARD. That is the whole reason for doing this. If your man is broke and out of work and you bury him in the back yard; he's gonna stay home but his ass will stay broke and out of work too!

If you have a really good job and you want to hang on to it then you can do a work and bury it behind the house to keep your job nailed down. I know this may be confusing but use your common sense. You ALREADY have success, money a good job. The key words here are ALREADY HAVE! This is why it is important to have hands on training so you can be taught what to do and when to do it if you are going to claim to be a PROFFESIONAL WORKER! You are dealing with the lives of folks that are desperate for help.

EXAMPLE 2

When is it safe to bury or throw in the back yard or in the West? Any time you want to remove something from you or hold something down. I'm going to give a few examples.

If you have a co-worker and you both want the same job, you can bury them behind your house or in the West and this will always keep them behind you. They want be able to move forward.

If bill collectors are hounding you, put them behind you! Bury them behind the house or in the West. Petition and pray that they be removed.

IN THE EAST

The sun rises in the East so anything that you are trying to bring to you should be buried, thrown or worked in the East. The East is easy to understand; internet workers don't understand how to work with the West or behind the house. I hope I have cleared this up for some who have been giving bad advice. Sorry to be so blunt but this kind of stuff pisses me off. If you are going to put yourself out there as a PROFFESIONAL ROOTWORKER then you need to know what the hell you are doing.

WASHES AND WATERS

Spiritual bathes are a very important part of Conjure. They are an important part of any magic work. During our daily lives we are around many different people, some of these people have negative energy all over them. We as living beings attract that energy, if we don't spiritually cleanse ourselves that negative energy clings to us. Over time it will build. Any time we pray, chant, light a candle or put forth our will other entities are drawn to that power. Some of them may not have your best in mind. For this reason it is important to have some kind of cleansing regiment in place; this can be achieved by brushing yourself down with a candle, a broom, a Chicken Foot, a feathered fan or you can take a spiritual bath. This needs to be done before and after you do your work. You don't want to bring unwanted energies into your work or hold on to anything you might have drawn to you during your work.

Sometimes when all this negative energy builds up things start going wrong in our lives; this will continue to go on until we cleanse ourselves. I have had clients who have come to me positive that they had been crossed. After doing a reading for them it turned out that it was nothing that a few spiritual bathes couldn't take care of. If you find yourself in this position try taking at least three spiritual bitter bathes; then three sweet bathes. If the condition doesn't improve then find a worker who can give you a reading to look further into the problem. Not only must we keep our bodies spiritually cleansed but we also need to keep our homes cleansed. If you do a lot of work in your home then you need to make sure you give your home a good spiritual cleansing at least once a month. One way to help protect your home from the folks who come in and out is to place a broom with the head facing upward behind the door. Negative energies love to hide in corners and out of the way places in our homes; our homes pick up the vibrations that are put out inside of them. If we don't clean all that mess out it just grows like a fungus.

It is also important that you keep your workspace spiritually cleansed. Energy builds and lingers. You should clean your altar area at least once a week. Even if you just sprinkle a wash or burn some incense. I know that now days we are all busy with life. But we need to be reasonable and responsible for the energies we draw into our homes. These energies spread to others who come in contact with our homes or us. They affect those around us. Spiritual bathes and washes are both made the same way. The only difference is one you bathe in and the other one you use in your mop water or as a sprinkle.

Most of the bathes and washes being sold today are not much more than colored water. I'm not even sure they are prayed over as they are being made. If you want a product to work it has to be filled with some type of prayer and petition or all you will have is some water; yes the roots and herbs hold some power but is it really enough to get a job done? I'm going to share with you the way I was taught to make a wash or bath. You need:

Five tea lights
A white handkerchief
A pot that can be used to steep your wash in

1. Lay out your handkerchief
2. Gather the herbs and roots you will need for your wash
3. Lay them out on your handkerchief
4. Set your tea lights around them in the shape of a cross
5. Set them top, bottom, right to left and light them
6. Set the fifth one in the center on top of the herbs and roots and light it
7. Hold your hands over your set up and pray your petition
8. Let your tea lights burn out
9. When the tea lights burn out gather up the handkerchief and hold it up to your mouth; pray your petition three times into the handkerchief then set it aside
10. Fill your pot with cool running water and set it on the stove
11. While the water is heating up say your petition and prayer over the water at least three times until it comes to a boil
12. When the water starts to boil turn the fire off
13. Add your roots and herbs to the water and pray your petition over the pot one more time before you cover the pot to let the mixture steep
14. Once the wash has cooled you can strain it
15. The roots and herbs can be put near the front door to draw in protection
16. Add a cup of the wash to your bath or to mop water to cleanse

I've listed some roots and herbs below in categories to help make it easy for you to make your own recipes. I want to give you a tried and true recipe that I was given in the 70's to cut and clear everything out of the way. It has never let me down.

1 cup strong black coffee
4 tbls Salt
1 cap Lemon Juice

1. Add the ingredients to the bath
2. Pray *Isaiah 41* and *Psalm 23* after each bath

Below is a small prayer that can be prayed over your wash. Since this is for cleansing I would say something like,

"Lord let this bathe or wash clear away all energies that don't belong, Lord cleanse me from head to toe, Let my mind be clear, Let my life be filled with light, Where there is light no darkness shall linger. Lord you said whatever is asked in your name shall be given. In the name of Jesus, I am cleansed!"

You can use any prayer you feel comfortable with. The important thing is that you pray. When you pray you need to stay focused on your petition and prayer. You need to put emotion into your prayers, make them heartfelt. What I'm trying to say is pour your heart out when you pray; call on whatever higher powers you believe in. There will be more about prayer a little later in the book. Below you will find a list of herbs that can be used in cleansing bathes. This is by no means a complete list; these are the ones I have found effective.

*A note of caution: Coffee, vinegar, and ammonia, strip away energy; they will strip away the good as well as the bad. Don't get heavy handed with them. Also if you put too much Mrs. Smith's bluing in the bath your skin will have a blue tint to it. Here a **little goes a long way.***

1 cup strong black coffee — strips away energy
1 capful ammonia — cleanses, protects, strips away energy
1 capful vinegar — cleanses, protects, strips away energy
1 capful Mrs. Smith

Eucalyptus — cleanses, protects
Rosemary — cleanses, protects
Rue — cleanses, protects
Hyssop
Bay leaves

All the Salts cleanse and protect but they also dry out your skin and your hair. If you decide to use Salt just a pinch prayed over will do the trick. Salt is a mineral and can be charged just like a crystal can be.

Remember when you take a spiritual bathe you need to make sure your head gets cleansed also. This is very important. You also need to pray while you are in the bath. Any three herbs from the list above will make a good cleansing bath. I personally like coffee, Salt, and ammonia. That is the combination I use most of the time but you use what you want too. Use whatever works for you.

You also need to remember when you do cleansing bathes you need to replace the negative energies you removed. You should follow up with a set of sweetening bathes or dress yourself with some type of spiritual oil.

You don't want to leave yourself open; the empty space will be filled with some other type of energy. When I make a sweetening bathe for myself I like to use a drop of honey and a pinch of Sugar don't get heavy handed with them or you will come out of the bath all sticky. A little goes a long way. I also like to use a white rose in my sweetening bathes. Rue is one of my favorite herbs, it not only cleanses but it also protects you. When an herb has a dual purpose I charge it with the intent of the work I'm doing. Last but not least is High John; I call this the wonder root. This root will do almost anything you ask it too. Below you will find a small list of bitter herbs and ones that can be used for sweetening. This is by no means a complete list of either.

BITTER HERBS

Some of these are not herbs but they can be used to strip away negative energy.

Strong Black Coffee	Basil
Vinegar	Sage
Ammonia	Myrrh
Limes	Rosemary (for women)
Lemons	Dragons Blood
Garlic	Frankincense
Cloves	A pinch of Ginger
Rue	Eucalyptus
Hyssop	Tobacco
Rock Salt	Allspice

SWEET HERBS

Honey	Five-Finger grass
Sugar	Roses
Powder Sugar	Lavender
Syrup	Sunflowers
Cinnamon	Rue
Mint	Salt
Chamomile	High John
Marjoram	

As I said this is not a complete list of bitter and sweet herbs, this list can be used to give you an idea what to use for your cleansing and sweetening bathes. As always use what works for you. Make sure you empower your herbs with prayer, before you add them to your bathe.

CONJURE WATERS

When I was a young at least once a year the church would go down to the creek. Everyone would stand in the water's edge and of course there were baptisms, then the preacher would bless everyone in the water. I think that sometimes we don't think about how powerful water really is. When we're parched it soothes us, after a hard day's work it refreshes us, when our feet hurt a good soak with some Salts makes us feel like heaven. There's nothing like standing in nice cool water and just letting it flow over your feet and ankles.

There are many different waters worked with in Conjure. I think that the different waters can be put in loose categories. This is not written in stone, you can use them any way you want to. To figure out what type of water you need for a job you have to first decide your goal. What are you trying to achieve with the work? You find the water that will be helpful in your work by looking at the elements of the water. You have to use your common sense; you wouldn't use hurricane or lightening water for a Blessing Water. You have to think about the cause and effect of the water. Below is a list of the different kind of water that can be worked with in Conjure and a notation of how it can be used.

Holy Water — healings, blessings, uncrossing, protection
Tar Water — uncrossing and protection, kills tricks
Ocean Water — cleansings and blessings
Spring Water — refreshing to the spirit
Creek Water — refreshing to the spirit
Rain Water — refreshing to the spirit
River Water — to remove something or someone away from us
Storm Water — to stir things up
Lightening Water — to heat up the work or cross up
Hurricane Water — to get things moving or to cross up
Stagnant Water — to cross up
Tar Water or Creolina

Tar water is like a double edge sword; it can be used for cleansing and protection but it can also be used in crossing works. Today we are looking at it for cleansing and protection. It's hard to find tar now days but you can find Creolina which is a commercial brand sold in some ole stores. Creolina is a coal tar deodorant cleaner it can be used to spiritually cleans the inside and the outside of the house.

This stuff smells really bad but it works. Just a cap in a mop bucket or in a spray bottle can be used to cleanse the house. If you mop your house make sure you clean the corners. Once you have mopped the whole house take the left over mop water and pour it at the end of your walk way in a straight line. This will put a straight line of protection across your walk way; if anything or anyone tries to cause you issues they have to cross that spiritual line.

Creolina mixed with a little Holy Water and Salt can offer an added protection to your yard. Make a bucket up and dress the 4 corners of the yard and around the house. Creolina will also kill any tricks that have been thrown in your yard. You can also wash your door, stoop and sidewalk down once a week to bring in blessings. This stuff smells really bad and you have to be careful because it can burn the skin. Never work with it unless you have added water to it. This may seem like simple work but it is powerful.

HOLD AN ENEMY DOWN

There are times when folks just don't know when to stop or they cause harm to others without a second thought. This is a simple but very powerful work that will stop them and hold them down, it also brings justice. This is not the type of work that you just go around throwing; if you are not justified in doing this work and they try to do a reversal you may find yourself being held down. Stagnate water is very powerful when you are doing crossing work. This type of water is basically "sour" water. To an ole school Conjure worker this means it can sour the target and hold them down because stagnate water has no movement to it.

There are a few ways this water can be used in your work. One is to add it to a jar work, the other is to drop a jar work into a pool of stagnate water either way is a powerful work.

Take Judges 16 V 27-31 out of an ole Bible.
Write the targets name on it;
cover that with your petition and place it in a jar.

The rest of the ingredients depend on you and just how far you want to take your *"justice"*.

Once you have all the ingredients in the jar you can either fill the jar with the water and work it daily or you can close the jar tie a string around the jar and place it in a pool of stagnate water. This way you can find the jar and remove it from the water when you feel justice is served or you can just leave it in there forever.

BLESSING WATER

Have you ever just stood in the rain during a good rain shower and let the water just wash over you. It makes you feel revived and cleansed. You can still get that effect.

1. Collect some rain water; try to catch it when it isn't storming just a hard rain
2. Bring it to a boil
3. Add:
   A pinch of Salt
   Bay Leaf
   A couple of drops of Lemon Juice
4. Let it steep like you would if you were making a cup of tea
5. Once it is steeped and cooled you can use this as a rinse for your head

This will make your head refreshed and if there is anything there it will be removed.

6. Let your hair air dry and don't forget to dress your head

Ocean Water

The only time I would work with ocean water is for cleansing work or to punish my enemy. Let me explain; because of the ebb and flow of the ocean it is not good to do prosperity work or love work. It is perfect for all types of enemy work.

1. You can make a Conjure jar for your target
2. Throw it in the ocean

When the tide comes in they will feel the power of the work. When the tide goes out they will have relief because the work will have moved away from them.

This is an on-going work, the target will think the work is gone but then it will hit them again as the tide comes in.

Hotfoot

Collect some River Water
To it add the picture of your target
Red Pepper
Sulfur
Some red ants.

1. Work the jar for five days
2. Then throw it in a river away from your home

Your target will soon be moving like the river away from you.

TINCTURES

The art of tincture making is being lost in Conjure work. You don't hardly ever hear workers now days talking about making tinctures. Tinctures are powerful spiritual waters made with an alcohol base. In the old days they used vinegar to make tinctures. The alcohol or vinegar will draw the spirit from the herb you are using. Tinctures can be worn as perfume, used as a sprinkle, added to bathes or washes; they can also be taken as a tonic. If you are interested in making your own tinctures here are a few easy steps you can follow.

1. Powder your herbs
   you can do this by using a coffee grinder.
2. Place your herbs in a canning jar
3. Fill the jar with your liquid to about two inches from the top of the jar

You need to allow room for air build up.

4. Seal the jar tightly and then shake the jar well then put it in a dark place
5. You can wrap the jar in tin foil to keep the light out
6. Shake the jar a couple of times a day for about a month
7. When the month is up strain the liquid from the herbs into a clean jar; use a white handkerchief to catch the herbs
8. Once you have all the herbs collected, ring the hankie until all the liquid is out of the herbs
9. Place the seal tightly on the jar, then label the jar

Remember this is a spiritual tincture and your petition and prayers need to be said during the whole process. The tinctures will last a long time.

Here are a few of my recipes.

UNCROSSING

Angelica Root
Saltpeter
Lemon Grass
Devil's Bit
Marjoram

ROAD OPENER

High John
Solomon Seal
Rose Mary
Rue
Blackberry

CUT AND CLEAR

Rue
3 lemons (cut and squeezed)
Angelica Root
Saltpeter
Master of the Woods

TO DRAW GOOD LUCK AND PROSPERITY

Cinnamon sticks
Five Finger Grass
Devil's Shoe string
Blue Flag
Magnet

Brooms

I love brooms! I always have since I was big enough to sweep with one. There is a lot of superstition about brooms; is it really superstition? Broom straw plucked from a new broom then bound together in the shape of a cross placed over the door will protect the home. If you are around my home and the broom falls you will hear a chorus of voices say "broom fell company is coming" I can't ever remember not hearing that. If you sweep over someone's feet either the law will be drawn to them or an argument is coming. It depends on who is around as to which superstition you hear. You hear folks talking all the time about sweeping things out of their houses; what about sweeping things in. I learned this at a young age.

About 6 or 7 years ago I was giving some classes at a shop whose business was not doing well. The classes were helping but folks just weren't spending their money in the shop. I told the

shop owners about a trick I learned a long time ago to sweep money into the house. Basically you throw change and bills in the door way then using a broom you sweep it into the shop or home while praying that you are prosperous. Needless to say they had a record sales day. This really works.

If you are bringing money into the home start on the side walk or near the road and sweep it towards your home. This will bring money in.

The broom can be used to cleanse away crossed conditions by brushing yourself off with it from head to toe.

If you want to stop haunts from bothering you at night place a broom across the door of your bedroom.

If you want to let your dead reach you in your dreams place a photo of them on the broom head and put the broom under your bed; you will dream of them.

Sweeping the yard from back to front will kill any tricks that have been thrown in the yard.

There is much more but I think this is enough food for thought for right now. You won't look at the broom the same.

JUMPING THE BROOM

During slavery times a slaves marriage didn't have a legal standing nor was the marriage protected from the abuses and domination imposed on them by the slave-owners. A married couple, who were slaves were without legal rights, they could be separated or sold at their owners will. If the couple resided on different plantations they were allowed to visit each other only if they had their owners' permission. They were not allowed to live in the same house hold like white married couples were. They didn't have the benefit of being married by the church. Historian John Blassingame wrote about this. In his writings he states:

> "that in most cases the slaves had to simply get their master's permission. Then they would move into a cabin together."

House servants were often allowed to have a formal marriage. The slave-owner would have a preacher perform the ceremony. Often times there would be a large feast and dance held in the "quarters" to honor the couple's marriage. Often times the ceremony included the slave marriage ritual of *"jumping the broom"*. The couple would jump over a broomstick.

The custom of jumping the broom could vary from plantation to plantation. Jumping the broom was not a custom of slavery, but is a part of African culture. When slavery was over African-Americans could have church weddings. Most of them felt the broom ceremony wasn't required anymore. Jumping the broom fell out of practice among most African Americans who wanted nothing to do with anything associated with the slavery. A lot of practices were put aside. When Black folks moved to the North they wanted nothing to do with the practices of the South that they thought were back-wards. Many became interested in their heritage when Alex Haley published his book "Roots". Jumping the Broom is also practiced who are not African American.

There are different religions that practice this ceremony within their culture. To name a few Wiccans and Gypsies have developed their own broom-jumping tradition.

The broom has always had a spiritual value; it symbolizes the sweeping away past wrongs or removing evil spirits. When a couple jumps over the broom in a wedding they are leaving the past behind them. They are beginning a new life together. They are becoming one in their marriage. I wanted to write about this because I think it is a very important ceremony and two because I have the honor of making my soon to be daughter- in-laws broom for her wedding to my son.

BROOMS FOR CLEANSING

I have used the broom for cleansings and protection for many years. The broom is one of my favorite tools to work with for a quick cleansing. The use of the broom in Conjure work is being lost due to the fact that these so called teachers that are out there don't know how you work with the broom. They can't explain how to use it in cleansings so they just mention it but not how to work with it. The broom is used for sweeping so therefore it can literally sweep a crossed condition off of you. The broom can not only be used for uncrossing but it can also be used for protection. I'm going to give you a few different works that can be used by working with the broom. This is old work that is being lost and needs to be remembered.

Now days you can find many different sizes of brooms; for this type of work you need a medium to a small broom. When you use a broom in cleansing work it is called either sweeping or brushing. I have a few different brooms that I use in my cleansings. I think my favorite is the old timey whisk broom I use. It's the kind folks use to use to sweep their cars out with before we had vacuum cleaners. I'm telling my age now. You can still find them at some of the old auto parts houses. I like this type of broom because it is small and they are put together well. You can use whatever you have; but the broom should only be used for this type of work.

Once you find the broom you will work with you need to cleanse it before you use it. I have a wash I use to spray my brooms down with, don't soak it just mist it lightly with a spray. Let the broom air dry; once it is dry sprinkle a little kosher Salt on it. Let the Salt sit on the broom until you are ready to use your broom.

To use the broom for cleansing you start at the crown of your head and sweep downward while praying that whatever is there is swept away. You sweep the bottom of your feet also from heel to toe. Make sure you sweep your whole body and you really need to focus on your head. When someone crosses you up that is main part of the body they hit. When you are finished brushing yourself down then lightly spray the broom down with a cleansing wash and let it dry. The next time you want to use it, the broom will be dry.

Floor Sweeps

Growing up we had hard wood floors. I remember our house always smelled nice and it felt good. I'm using the word Floor sweep here because I think folks will understand it better, I was raised calling it "dusting". If you called anyone of my siblings or my children or grandchildren and asked them what was good to remove problems from the home they would all tell you coffee grounds. My daughter would tell you to sprinkle coffee grounds from back to front while praying and let it sit for a while. My brother would tell you to take the morning coffee grounds squeeze a little Lemon Juice into them let them dry then sprinkle them throughout the house. My mama would have added a little soda to that.

Coffee grounds will cut and clear anything that is disturbing the household. It will also get rid of any odors.

Pine straw gathered in the west side of the house, then sprinkled on the floor will remove all crossed conditions placed on the house. Start from back to front early in the morning before the dew dries; leave it on the floors until the sun begins to set. Then sweep it out the door to the road.

Rose Mary and soda make a good cleansing sweep. It also keeps the woman of the house in charge. My mama kept rose pedals and soda under her bed to keep peace in the bedroom. She would sweep it out of the house once a week and put fresh down.

You can place Lavender and soda under your furniture in your home to ensure peace and blessings. Change it once a week placing it in the East side of your yard.

Floor sweeps are old Conjure remedies to keep the home running smooth.

MONEY SWEEP

You can make a money sweep to draw money into your home.

1. Take a pinch of dirt from the four corners of the cross road nearest you
2. Add:
   A pinch of dirt from your door stoop
   Mix this dirt with a pinch of Powdered Sugar
   Salt
   Powdered Cinnamon
   A little shredded money in the mix

To lay the sweep down:

1. Start at the front door make a trail of the mixture through the house
2. Pray for prosperity to be swept into your home
3. Let the mixture sit for a little while
4. Then start at the front door and sweep your trail all the way to the back door
5. Gather up the powder and place it in the center of the crossroads

CONJURE BALLS

Conjure balls can be made from wax, crawdad mound, dirt from the graveyard or crossroads and clay. As the ball dries it draws the work and makes it stronger. These little balls can be used for many things, from drawing money to crossing up an enemy. There is much to making them but they sure are powerful to be a little ball. Below you will find a few recipes to make your own.

HEALING CONJURE BALL

You need:

> The hair from the crown of the person head that is ill
> A small Lodestone
> For this ball use Clay

1. Roll out the clay into a patty

2. Place the Lodestone and hair in the center the roll the patty into a ball
3. Wrap the ball in a white handkerchief
4. Tie one knot in the handkerchief
5. Take the packet and wipe the person who is ill down from head to toe
6. Have them blow three breathes into the packet
7. Repeat the process as many times as possible daily

As the clay dries the illness will dry up

8. When the person is well bust the ball apart; give them their hair back
9. Clean the Lodestone with some cool running water and Whiskey
10. Throw the clay in the crossroads.

CONFUSION CONJURE BALL

There are times when we need to get control of a situation. This could be a troublesome person on our job or someone who just keeps dogging us. For this Conjure Ball you need to use *"Crawdad Mud"*.

Get a photo of the target and burn it to ash
Mix the ash with the Crawdad Mud

1. Make a patty and place a nail in the center
2. Then add:
   Sulfur
   Gunpowder
   Black Mustard Seeds
   A dried Habanera Pepper Pod
3. Roll your patty into a ball.

Make sure you are making your petition against your target as you are making the Conjure Ball.

4. Set the ball on a plate and poke a black stick candle in the center of the Conjure ball

5. Keep up the heat until you get your results
6. Then you can throw the Conjure ball in the graveyard or in running water

PROTECTION BALL

This work is the combination of working with a Conjure ball, and a packet. The concept of the work is to protect yourself if someone is trying to cross you up. The way it works is anytime someone tries to throw at you, the ball or head will take the hit. Any enemies or spirits working against you will think they are hitting you, when in truth the packet is taking all the hits. It does so because it's linked with your spirit. Most of the time when an enemy lays a trick the area that will be affected first is your head. The reason this is done is because it causes confusion and you won't realize you are being hit.

The ball works the same way a doll baby would because you use your personal items to link the work to your spirit. Most workers I know use some type of link to their target. This could be a photo, or any personal item they may have. These items are used to build a bridge between their work and your spirit. Due to all the social networking sites such as Facebook it is easy to get a picture of a target or they can even work with your name and date of birth on a petition paper. The protection ball will work as a stand-in for you; because it is filled with your spirit and personal items. It will protect you from being hit by your enemies, and the ball will destroy any work being done on you. It will confuse any spirits that are sent to attack you at night while you are sleeping; they will be drawn to the packet instead of you.

For the packet you need:

A white handkerchief
Dirt from a church
Devil's Bit
Master Root
Master of the Woods
Dirt Daubers Nest *(to confuse your enemies)*

This work needs to be done every night for nine nights before you go to sleep.

1. Start at the crown of your head and wipe yourself going downward with the white handkerchief.
2. As you wipe yourself downward call on the Holy Trinity; say:

   "In the name of the Father, In the name of the Son and In the name of the Holy Ghost I am cleansed!"

3. Repeat this for nine days
4. You can either tie the handkerchief on you at night or you can place it in your pillow either way will work
5. Once you have finished your nine nights spread the handkerchief out on a table.
6. Place all of your ingredients in the center of the handkerchief
7. Set your tea lights top, bottom, right, left, and then place the fifth on top of your ingredients
8. Place your hands over the set up and call the Trinity and ask them to place a fiery wall of protection around you that will not be broken
9. Let your lights burn out; try to pray over your set up at least three times during the burning
10. After the tea lights burn out you need to make a packet out of the handkerchief by folding it and the ingredients away from you
11. Place your packet on a square of Red Flannel
12. Fold the Red Flannel towards you pray to the Trinity for protection
13. Cover yourself with the Blood of Jesus
14. Pray that all work sent against you is covered with the Blood of Jesus and cannot succeed
15. As you began to wrap your packet pray *Jeremiah 1:18-19*

18 Today I have made you a fortified city, an iron pillar and a bronze wall to stand against the whole land against the kings of Judah, its officials, its priests and the people of the land.

19 They will fight against you but will not overcome you, for I am with you and will rescue you," declares the LORD.

16. Wrap the packet up using red cotton; wrap going one way then turn the packet and wrap going the other way.
17. As you wrap the thread around the packet pray, petition the Trinity to trap any evil that is not of God into the packet.

Make sure you wrap the thread tight so the packet won't come undone.

18. Tie the thread off with five knots
19. Feed the packet with Whiskey and Fiery Wall of Protection Oil
20. Once a week hold the packet up to your mouth, call on the Trinity and pray your petition into the packet
21. Place your packet in the cross set up to feed it
22. Give it a little Whiskey to keep the spirit of protection fed
23. Place the packet under your side of the bed for total protection during the night while you sleep

CHICKEN FEET

The Chicken Foot is a wonderful tool to use for cleansing. Chickens are well known for their ability to scratch and peck for their food. My grandma had a coop full of hens and two roosters when I was growing up. I was fascinated by them, I still am. She didn't always keep them locked up in the coop, at least once a week they got out to scratch and peck in the yard. It is well known that the chicken scratches up messes! This one reason their feet work so well in cleansing. By scratching yourself lightly with a Chicken Foot you will be removing the negative energy from yourself. Just like the chicken scratches. If you don't have time to do a cleansing bath here is another way to remove things from you. This will remove jinx conditions, crossed conditions or anything else that may have been put on you or that you have attracted. The Chicken Foot works because chickens are known to scratch up all types of messes. This is simple but very effective way to cleanse one's self. All you need is a dried Chicken Foot, and the first verse of *Psalm 23*.

1. You start at the top of your head going downward lightly scratch yourself with the Chicken Foot
2. While you are doing this say the first verse of *Psalm 23.*

3. Make sure that you do your feet also, going from heel to toe
4. Once you have made one pass over your body with the Chicken Foot, and then turn one full circle around turning counter-clockwise

By turning counter-clockwise you will be unraveling whatever is left that the Chicken Foot didn't get.

5. If you are removing a crossed or jinxed condition you would do this for nine nights in a row

This may seem like a strange way to cleanse one's self, but I was taught this many years ago. I was twenty-one when I was first shown this and vey ill while I was carrying my daughter. The black lady my family hired to stay with me taught me how to do this. She was a very special person whom I came to love dearly. Though she has passed on, I think of her often. This is old Conjure work, it really does work and it works fast. Now I want to give you instructions on how to dry your own chicken feet.

You can find raw chicken feet at most small markets. I dry from a half a dozen to a dozen at a time because it takes so long to dry them.

1. You need to wash them in cool running water once you get them
2. I just pat them dry

There are two ways to dry them.

3. You tie a string on them one at a time don't bunch them together and hang them up outside to sun dry

The only drawback to this is that the cats might get them. This is the fastest method to drying them.

The other method to dry them is to put them in rock Salt. This takes about a month for them to dry. I have tried to put them in the oven on a very low heat but that didn't work, so the above methods are the only two I know of to dry them.

To dry them in rock Salt you need:

A bowl with a tight lid on it
A box of rock Salt

1. Cover the bottom of the bowl with the Salt
2. Then place your chicken feet on the bed of Salt
3. Shape the claws on the foot the way you want them
4. Then cover the chicken feet with more Salt

You can make layers if you have too.

5. Close the lid tightly and put them up in a dark place. It can take anywhere from a month to six weeks to dry them. It depends on how much fat they have on them
6. Once they are dry brush the Salt off of them, DO NOT wash them
7. Then you dress them light with oil and pray over them.

DOLLIES

The making of doll babies is ancient; their use today is similar to the way they were used in the old days. I think in the old days the dolls were made by the slaves to have some control over their lives. The way these people had to live and were treated was beyond cruel. Poor white folks were just a step above them, the rich of the time ruled with a cruel fist. These folks brought with them a knowledge that white folks could not begin to understand; and I'm sure they feared them. I think in those days Dollies were made with anything they could find.

These folks didn't have money; hell they were lucky to have food in their bellies! I'm no scholar; but my mama was born and raised in South Carolina. I grew up on stories of the old days. I lived there myself; my only daughter was born in South Carolina in the early 70's. I think to really understand Conjure you have to understand the people. I want to give you a brief history of my family and what I know for a fact. My mama was the baby of eight children. My Granddaddy had crippling arthritis and couldn't work in the fields. That left my Grandma and her children to go to work. One of my uncles had polio as a child and couldn't work either. I have a picture of my grandparents sitting in the door way of the shack my mama was raised in.

My mama took me there when I was in my teens; what I saw shocked me. This place was nothing but a shell of a house. Mama told me they used to have to stuff rags and news paper in the cracks and holes to keep the wind out in the winter time. The house was in the woods set away from the main house. My mama and Grandma worked in the cotton and tobacco fields right along with the blacks. They were treated no better than the black folks they worked with. My own summers were filled by working under the tobacco barn; I even worked in the fields sometimes. I never had to pick cotton; thank God. You form a bond with folks that you work with from day light until dark; the South is a whole different world from the rest of the country. Outsiders are kept at arm's length; but folks who belong there can always go home. All of my Mama's people are from South Carolina.

I'm sure that in the old days, whatever could be found was used to make Dollies. I know of three types that I have not seen people talk about. One is the corn cob Dollie. There is a story behind this doll and how I know about it.

When I was caring my daughter I was very ill. I was put on bed rest for five months. My Grandma knew this lady and asked her to come to my house and help me during the week. She treated people who were ill. I think that due to her efforts my daughter is alive today. I trusted her because my Grandma trusted her. I was only twenty-one at the time. She prayed over me every day; one day she asked if she could have some of my hair. She could have just taken the hair from my brush, at this time my hair was very long. She told me the hair needed to come from the crown of my head.

A few days later she came with this Dollie. This was the first time I had ever seen a doll like this. The body of the doll was a corn cob and the doll was covered in corn husk. When I asked her what it was for all she told me was to keep me and my baby safe. After I had my daughter the Dollie disappeared. When I asked her about the missing doll she told me the doll wasn't needed anymore. I have never seen another Conjure doll like that one again.

One time I was digging in my Grandma's room and found what I thought was just a small old rag doll. I got my butt spanked good for that one. Something's you never forget. The doll was made out of rags and had button eyes; but the funny thing was that the mouth was sewn shut. There was three X's sewn over the mouth. I now know that the doll was made to shut someone's mouth. The doll was male, because it had on cover all's. I don't know for sure but I think it was made for the man who owned the farm my Grandma worked on.

When I was about twelve I was helping my favorite Aunt clean out the chest a drawers in the spare room she had. I found a stick doll that had a dried apple for a head. The doll had on clothes just like my uncle wore, the legs of the pants was stuffed with cotton. I thought this doll looked really weird and I really didn't want to touch it. The head gave me the creeps. I remember asking my Aunt how the head got all swiveled up and she told me in the oven. At twelve this sounded crazy to me. For once I didn't ask any more questions.

I have often thought about that apple head doll. I even asked my cousin if she had found the doll after my Aunt had passed. She didn't know what I was talking about. I think that this type of Dollie would be wonderful for love Conjures or even money Conjures. I'm going to try and make one; if I succeed you will find a picture of the doll later on in this book. With the full instructions on how the doll was made.

By the time I learned how to make Conjure dolls Red Flannel was the material that most workers used. As a rule I try to work as traditional as possible; but if I am out of something I will find something else to use. I don't let that stop me if I have a job that needs to be done. If I have personal clothing of the person I am making the doll to represent I prefer to use that material to make the doll with. Then I will wrap the doll in a Red Flannel packet. No two workers work the same and since I am writing about how I work, the information given here will reflect that.

Each worker works different; we all have had different teachers. I don't want to get mail that say's so and so told me to make a Dollie this way; are they wrong? No they are not wrong! I do stand firm on the fact that a factory made doll will not hold the power that a doll you have made yourself or had a worker make for you will have. Dolls are used for many different situations; they are not always used for dark work. It seems now days most folks think that the doll baby is used to curse or cross someone up; this is not all a doll baby can be used for. The doll baby can be used for healing; protection, money drawing, and yes darker Conjure. You won't find the darker parts of Dollie work in this book. I feel that in order to learn about that type of work you need to have hands on training, with a teacher who can show you how to do the work. The reason I take this stand is because that type of work can be dangerous, not only to the worker but also to the client.

Too many things can go wrong, if you have not had hands on training for the darker art of working with dolls. I have seen this happen and it has happened to me and my family. You will find some good works in this book. I am not all Sugary and nice when it comes to my work; but I can't be responsible for someone getting hurt because I gave instructions in this book where they could be harmed or harm an innocent bystander. I feel that every writer and teacher is responsible for the information they teach and write about.

I will try to explain in easy to understand words how to make and use doll babies in your work. So you and others around you will be safe. This type of work is not to be taken lightly; because it is very powerful work and can cause harm. I didn't gain my knowledge over night; I have worked almost forty years to get where I am. So take your time; don't try to do work you are not ready for. If you are interested in the darker part of doll Conjure then please find yourself a good teacher. Learn the right way.

The doll baby is a very powerful tool to help you achieve a goal. The Dollie is made to represent the person whom the work is being done on. This can even be one's self. Dolls are made for healing, protection, love work, enemy work and a variety of other works. Working with dolls is very serious work! You basically hold that persons spirit in your hands; if the doll is made right. There is so much information out there on Dollies but none of it really tells you how to work with the dolls; or warns you about the care you must give the doll once the doll is named. This worries me; I have always believed that if you are going to give information then give all the information that is needed in order for the work to be completed. Anyone can give instructions on how to put a Dollie together and the ingredients that go into the doll; but what next?

You always need a link to the person the Dollie represents; this can be a picture, personal items or a petition paper. Don't ever put a doll together without adding something that identifies the person the doll represents inside the doll. I never tell people that anything is written in stone; but I am now. Let me explain why; let's say I am furious with one of my son's, I'm mad as hell at him but I need to do some work on my husband. Some issue has come up and I need to act now! So I decide to make a Dollie of my husband to do what work needs to be done; but I am still furious at my son.

I clear my mind (I think) and I began working on the Dollie. I don't think I need anything personal or a petition because I have named the doll for my husband and the spirit will go where I tell it to go. Do you honestly believe this? Even though I am focused on my husband my subconscious is still focused on my son. I have taken a chance here with my son. I don't know about all of you but I am not that good. I can't over ride my subconscious. This is why it is so important that you have something that links that doll to the person the doll represents. Naming the doll is not enough; you need at least a petition with the person's name on it.

Once the doll is made and named it is important that as you work with the doll you use the person's name that the doll represents. This helps remind the spirit of the person you are working on that the doll is that person. Reparation is very important in this type of Conjure. I have found over the years that just naming a doll is not enough; you have to add something that links that doll to the person. This is one reason I recommend that you make your own doll babies; because as you put the Dollie together you are focused on the person the doll is being made for, this adds power to the doll.

When I decide I need to put a doll together the first thing I do is:

1. A cleansing on myself

I don't want anything that is going on with me to bleed over into this work. I usually just brush myself down with either a chicken wing or the buzzard wing I have.

2. Then I dress my head and my hands; because they are the ones that do the work
3. Once I have myself ready I pray and ask God to lead me to the right ingredients that will make this work a success
4. From this moment on I play the person's name over and over in my mind until I have everything gathered I need to make the doll baby
5. As I gather the items I lay everything out on my work space; when I have everything I need I pray over everything in the person's name the doll is being created for

You need everything linked to the target. I don't cut the doll out until all of this is done.

As we all know knots hold power, when you tie a knot it can't be broken; if you want to undo the knot you have to cut it. Scissors cut magic. When I make a doll I use knots to add power to the doll. I like to use five knots sometimes; this represents the crossroads. Other times I will use thirteen or twenty-one knots.

6. J tie the knots on the hands, feet and head of the doll.

This is another step that adds power to the doll and when you call the name of the doll.

7. As you tie off each knot call the person's name and state your petition.

This is how I was taught to make a doll baby. Don't use scissors to cut the thread because this will cut the work; don't use your teeth either you will mix your personal concerns into the work, just break the thread.

8. J personally like to stuff the head of the doll with the items J am using.

This is how I was taught and the way I have always done the work. The only time I don't do this is if one I am doing hotfoot work and two if I am doing love work. If the work is too hotfoot someone then:

1. J place the hotfoot powder in the feet
2. Everything else goes in the head

If I am doing love work then:

1. The magnet or Lodestones and Pyrite go over the heart area
2. Everything else goes in the head
3. J name each Lodestone or magnet , Petition the Pyrite to draw the two people together; J then soak the stones in a attraction oil before J add them to the heart area

I try to stay as traditional as I can in my work. The only materials I use for my Dollies are:

Flannel
Something belongings to the target

If I use something that belongs to the target

4. I wrap the doll in a flannel packet
5. If you are making a rag doll then you could add the personal material and flannel tied on the frame of the doll

I don't use moss in my doll babies that I make; I was taught that moss is used when you want to jinx someone. Like I have said a million times not all workers work the same; this is how I work! So, if *so and so* uses moss and it works for them then that is the right way for them to make their dolls. It's not my place to tell another worker how to do their work; like I said this is my book and my works so the work here will be written the way I work.

When I make a stick doll I use two different types of sticks. Sometimes I will use both types of sticks on the same doll; it all depends on the work.

I use oak sticks — because the oak tree holds power and is strong

Or

I use Licorice Sticks — for their dominating power.

Once I have the frame of the doll put together I cover the body with flannel. I will explain in more detail in the section of the book called stick doll. Before we move on to making the doll's I want to give a **Note of caution**:

Please be **very careful** when you do Doll Baby Conjure.
Make sure you are focused on the work at hand.
Be sure that you cleanse yourself before you start the work; you don't want the work to backfire on you.

If this is the first time you have done this type of work then try something simple.

Don't jump in with both feet!

Some Sage advice that was given to me many years ago;

Don't ever work when you are mad unless it is the target you are working on.

Even then use caution in what you say and do while working.

I'm not preaching we each have to do what we feel is right; just make sure that what you do you can live with.

Naming the Doll Baby

Once you have your doll baby put together then it is time to name the baby. I was taught two ways to do this. One is to use Holy Water from the Catholic Church; this is the method I prefer. The other is to add Kosher Salt to water and bless the water. Either way will work. You hold the baby in your left hand and sprinkle the water on the baby while naming the Dollie.

> "I call on God the Father,
> God the son,
> and God the Holy Spirit.
> I ask of you God most high
> that this doll represents _____.
> From this time, in this moment,
> this doll will be alive.
> Everything that is done to this doll,
> will be done too _____
> until at which time I decide to release them.
> I command you O Doll,
> made with these hands that you come to life,
> In the name of God most high!
> Amen"

Once you have your doll named then you can start to work on the doll. Please, use common sense when doing this type of work. I can't stress this enough.

Stick Dolls

Most of the time I make either cloth dolls or wax dolls; there have been times when I have made stick dolls. It really depends on the work and what I have on hand. To me making a stick doll is double the work; but sometimes this is the better doll to use in some types of work. I want to touch on the two types of stick dolls I make. These are the only two types of wood I use:

> One is made with Licorice Sticks;
> The other one is made out of oak.

I like to use oak in times when power is needed. Oak is very strong and the oak adds power to the doll and the work. I use Licorice Sticks when I am doing domination work.

The only drawback with using stick Dollies is that you have to make the head of the doll and the body has to be wrapped. If you have plenty of time then these dolls are worth the effort it takes to make them. They can be made ahead of time for different types of work if you want to keep them stocked. I prefer to make them as I go. It is really up to the worker.

I make the head of the dolls with:

> either Clay
> or Mud from a Crawdad hole

Both of these work well. The good thing about this is that you can add to the mixture as you work the clay or mud:

> Herbs
> Personal items
> Petition

Again there is a drawback because you have to let it dry.

1. I burn my Petition and add the ash to the Clay or Mud
2. Once I have the head made I stick the head onto my stick figure

3. Let it dry
4. Most of the time you will have to glue the head on the figure once the head is dry

It takes a while to dry the head; I have at times placed the heads in the oven on a low heat to help the drying process.

5. I have found that to make the body of the doll it is easier to notch the sticks then put them together
6. I add a drop of glue to make them stable
7. Then wrap them with cotton thread

The color of the thread depends on the type of work I am doing.

8. If you want the doll to be padded then you can glue dressed cotton to the body of the doll or you can glue moss to the body depending on the purpose of the doll
9. Before you wrap the doll in Red Flannel or a piece of cloth that belonged to the person being worked on; make a wash with herbs and oils that pertain to the work
10. Pray over the wash and soak the material in the wash
11. Let the material dry then wrap your doll with the material

There have been times when I haven't wrapped my dolls. If I decide not to wrap them I write the person's name and DOB on the sticks. You can also do this before you wrap your doll.

Each of us work different and most of the time we find our own way of working. If you decide to make a stick doll you may find a different way that works better for you. If you do then try it and see how the work comes out.

CLAY DOLLS

Clay dolls are one of the easiest to make. They also hold a lot of power.

Of course clay dug out of the ground is the best to use for these dolls, but most of the time that is not possible. You can find molding clay at any craft store.

The clay doll is one of my favorite dolls to make. The good thing about making this type of doll is that you can focus on your petition the whole time you are molding the clay.

1. Make a wash and soak your herbs in the wash over night
2. Make sure you pray over the wash and state your petition

It is important to stay focused.

3. Strain the herbs and let them dry

It is important that they dry; if you don't let them dry all the way it will cause your doll to have mold. You can help the drying process by placing the herbs in the oven at a low heat. Be careful not to burn them.

4. Once the herbs are dry you can start to put the doll together
5. I always mix the herbs and my petition up with the clay. Keep working the clay until the clay becomes soft
6. It is at this time that you say your prayers and petition for the work
7. Once the clay is workable you can shape it into a human figure
8. When I am shaping the doll I call the person's name and talk to the person. This helps link the doll to the person
9. When you have the clay shaped you can either let the clay air dry or you can place the doll in the oven. Just be really careful not to burn the doll

If I am doing love work I place things in the heart area before I dry the doll.

> A **word of caution**; don't add a whole lot of herbs and such to the doll. If you over load the clay it want hold. The doll will crack.

This type of doll can be very powerful if it is made right. You can also use the mud from a crawdad hole for this type of doll. The only drawback is it takes longer to dry and when it dries it cracks. Other than that it works really well.

MAKING A WAX DOLL

You need a soft wax, the type of oil you choose to use, and herbs.

1. Just get the wax soft not melted
2. Then shape the wax into a small human figure.

I never worry if it looks like a male or female because I stay focused on my intent while making the doll. That's all you do!

WAX DOLL CHANT

Here is a short chant you can use when making your Dollie.

O creature of wax
I take from thee thy heart so cold
I replace it with the power of old.

Fire and water shall give spirit to thee
Earth and air, your form to be.

Be thou _____
In mind, body and soul
In my hands your life I hold.

Forever now, hearts beat as one.
This I say true,
and be it done!

There are many things that a wax doll can be used for. They can be used for healing, bindings, protection (for a person), reversal work, or whatever you are doing that represents a person. I use dolls quite a bit, for many different reasons. Some people think of this as dark magic, it is only dark if you use it that way. I believe there can't be light without dark. There has to be a balance in all things. These are my thoughts and mine alone. The best dolls to work with are the ones you make yourself (Will explain below how to make a doll).

Be very cautious though, I'm not trying to scare you, but wax picks up your energy like a magnet and it holds on to it. That's why candle magic is so easy and successful. Now with that said, you can either choose the wax color by candle magic colors or you can either use white or black wax depending on what you are doing. I personally use only white or black wax. White is all colors and black can be used for many different purposes. From the moment you decide to make a doll you need to stay focused on what you will use it for. **NEVER** work with wax if you are upset, depressed, or ill, the wax will pick up those energies. By being focused on the outcome from the start you are charging your doll from the minute you pick up the wax.

EXAMPLE

Let's say you want to do a healing for a friend that is sick. You would need:

> White wax
> A few drops of Olive Oil
> Bay
> Rue
> Rosemary

1. You would then mix all the ingredients into the wax; while staying focused on your friend
2. Then shape the wax into a doll baby
3. Now you need to take some Holy Water and consecrate the doll, you would say something like:

   "I consecrate this doll in the name of God the Father, God the Son and God the Holy Spirit."

4. Make the sign of the cross over the poppet
5. Then you name the doll, you would say something like:

   "I call on God the Father, God the son, and God the Holy Spirit. I ask of you God most high that this doll represents _____. From this time in this moment this doll will be alive. Everything that is done to this doll will be done

too_____ *until at which time I decide to release them. I command you oh doll made of these hands that you come to life, In the name of God most high! Amen"*

6. Once you have the doll made you will need an altar that has been covered with a white cloth

7. Then make a bed out of the same herbs you used and place the doll on the bed. You will need:

Four brown eggs
A white candle
Olive Oil
A white Rosary

8. Take your white candle and anoint it with the Olive Oil in the name of Jesus *(or whatever higher power you choose to call on)*

9. Light the candle and pray that you be given the power you need to make this healing a success

10. Place the candle on the altar near the doll

11. Now you will take each of the eggs and using the Olive Oil make a cross on them; while saying:

"In the name of the God the Father, God the Son and God the Holy Spirit."

12. Once this is done you are ready to place the eggs; place one at the head of the poppet, one next to the right side, one to the left side and one at the dolls feet. You should have an egg placed at the head, feet, and at both sides

13. When this is done pick up the Rosary and the doll, while saying the prayer below wrap the Rosary around the doll; wrap it so the cross is laying on the dolls chest

"O Lord, the great Healer and good Physician, both of body and soul, who knowest our weakness and wilt not lay upon us more than we can bear, help us to bear it patiently.

Grant unto us who are sick and suffering, the aid of Thy heavenly healing. Lay upon our fevered brow cool fingers of Thy love and power.

May we who suffer now feel Thy love and power. May we who suffer now feel Thy presence within us, and the realization at this moment of Thy touch bringing to us new life, strength, and health.

Bless all who Thou hast called to minister to our afflicted bodies with skill and power; that they may exercise their art for our well being.

Hear us now as we pray for Thy healing touch. Thou who didst Thyself explore the vast treasure of pain on the cross, bestow upon us Thy grace.

We have known Thee as the Savior of our souls;

now we would know Thee as Savior of our bodies. We beseech Thee, that Thou mayest free us from all evil, and make us feel Thy presence even as we pray.

May we through suffering learn to love Thee better, for Jesus Christ's sake. Amen"

14. While still holding the poppet in your hands; in a strong commanding voice say:

    "This doll represents_____and their illness; as the Doll is healed so shall_____ be healed. In the name of God the father, God the Son, and God the Holy Spirit I pray."

15. Once this is done lay the doll on the bed of herbs

16. Give thanks for God's mercy

17. Then once a day you go to your altar and say the prayer over the doll

18. Once the person is healed you can give them the doll or you can unnamed the poppet and bury it under a tree with a small offering.

How to Dry an Apple Head

The first thing you need to do is buy some fresh apples, and Lemon Juice. Make sure the apples are not soft.

1. Make a wash of about one part water and two parts Lemon Juice

It has to be enough mixture to cover the apples.

2. Peal the apples, some folks like to carve the face; J didn't carve a face on mine, J let it make its own shape
3. Place the apple in the mixture for about twenty minutes
4. Remove the apple and pat the apple dry
5. Set the apple on a non stick cookie sheet; with the face looking at you
6. Bake in the oven for about five hours at 200 degrees

If you place the oven higher than 200 the apple will turn to mush.

7. Let the apple cool and take a small knife and bore a hole on top of the head

Be careful because the head will be really soft.

8. Load the head with the personal concerns and herbs
9. Replace the bit of apple you removed to cover the hole
10. Place the head back in the oven let it bake for a while longer
11. Then remove the head and put it in a dry place

By this time the head should be taking shape, I made the nose and eyes more defined by shaping them. I didn't want to cut a face out. I left the head out for three days so a lot of the Sugary juice could drain from the head.

12. Then I placed the head back in the oven to finish drying it

The drying process takes a good while, if you want to make this type of Dollie then dry more than one head at the time.

Side Note*

> Every once in a while take the apple out of the oven and reshape the face. I used my nails, because I didn't want to use a knife. Make sure you make a mouth on the doll head. As the head dries you will need to go back over the face so that it stays in shape. The apple will make a natural face as it is drying; you just have to refine the features. Remember to name the apple before you place it in the oven to dry, if you already have a use for the doll.

LOVE CONJURE DOLL

I made an apple head love doll out of the apple I dried. I decide to make this type of doll because I had someone who needed the doll. I wanted to make sure this doll would work before I added it too the book. I can't say who I made the doll for because that person will more than likely read this book; but I am going to tell you the steps I took and the great results the girl had that I gave the doll too. A family member came to me who was having trouble out of her husband. Now when I made the apple head it was just to test and see if I could. I didn't have a use for the doll at the time, so I didn't load the head.

The finished doll was made to bring a man home and to make him get a job. This family members husband wouldn't work, he was just plain lazy. She told him either get a job or get out! He got out. There was no contact for weeks. Finally she came to me for help.

Things Needed:

> Apple Head
> Small Lodestone
> Small Pyrite
> Petition/ Personal Items
> Master of the Woods
> Damiana
> Loveage
> 2 Licorice Sticks
> Red Flannel
> Sugar

1. Burn your petition paper to ash
2. Mix the ash with Master of the Woods, Damiana, Loveage and the Pyrite
3. Name the Lodestone for yourself so the person will think about you and be drawn to you

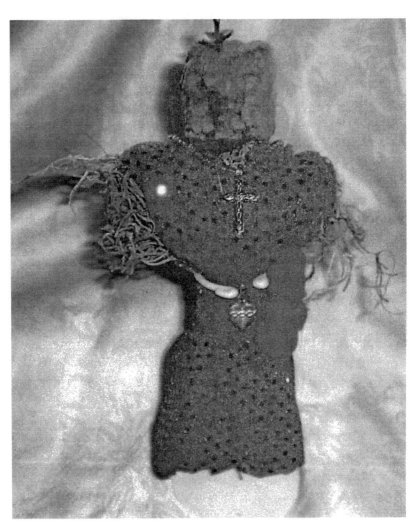

4. J placed all of this in the top of the apple head. Once J
   got the head ready J started on the body
5. Take the two Licorice Sticks and notch them, then place
   them together so they look like a stick figure
6. Use red thread to wrap around them so the arms and
   body will stay together

7. Tie the thread off with nine knots; call the person's name on each knot
8. If you want to you can just stop here and start to work the doll or you can dress the doll
9. For this doll I made a small shirt out of Red Flannel
10. I then soaked the shirt in the herb mixture and Sugar water
11. I put the shirt on my stick doll while it was wet; then I added the head

The Sugar water will make the shirt stiff.

12. After the shirt dried I named the doll then gave the doll to its owner

Within the week he was burning up her phone and is out looking for a job. So this type of doll works fast and gives results.

A LITTLE OF THIS AND THAT

HOW TO WRITE A PETITION

When I write out my petition I always date and sign the petition. You need to make sure your intent is clear. Here's an example of what I am talking about. Let's say I need a job, so I decide to do some work to help me find a job. If I write my petition out and state:

"I Want A Job"
or
"I want a job doing (whatever)"

Then I'll get just that a job. I may hate the job and not get along with my co-workers or my boss. Also this could be a job doing anything but; what if I change the wording of the petition?

Let's try the petition this way.

> *Date:* _____
>
> *Birth* _____
>
> *Name* _____
>
> *I want a job doing* _____.
> *I want to make more than enough money to make
> ends meet (or you can place the amount of pay you
> want to make). I want to be comfortable with my
> new boss and the people I work with. I want to be
> seen as a favorable asset to the company. I want
> a raise within* _____ *amount of
> time. I want this to be the perfect job for me.*
>
> *Signed* _____

You see from the example that you are stating exactly what it is you want from your new job. You want a job that you are good at and will be able to be promoted. Before I write out my petition I will sit down and think of what exactly it is I want to achieve. I may write it out three or four times before I get the wording right. Here's one more example.

Let's say you want to bring a new love into your life. You're ready to find someone who you can live with and be happy with. So you sit down and write out your petition.

> *"I want someone to love me. I want him to be crazy
> about me. He can't live without me. I want him to
> worship me; he will never look at another woman."*

What could be wrong with a guy like this, he would be perfect right? **WRONG!** This guy would drive you crazy; he would **suffocate** the life out of you. He would be so worried about what you are doing during the day he might not even work. He may even become **abusive**, why because he is so **nuts** about you. Do you see what I am getting at? How about if we wrote the petition this way?

Date: _____

Name_____

Birth _____

"I want a new mate brought into my life. Someone I am compatible with. Someone who is loving, caring and kind; Someone I can find true happiness with. Someone who is a good listener and will be interested in what I have to say. Bring me someone who will be a good provider, who will love, honor, and cherish me. Someone who will be supportive in whatever I may choose to do. Bring me someone I can live my life out with in peace and happiness.

Signed _____

Do you see the difference in the two petitions? You have achieved the same thing in both of them. Only in the second one you will get much more. Just take your time when you are writing out your petition, think before you leap. Make sure you know exactly what it is you are trying to achieve. It may seem like a lot of work, but the benefits are well worth the effort. You have to remember our higher power will try to bring us what we ask for. I want you to think before you write out your petition. By doing so you won't get something you didn't mean to ask for.

Petitions are a large part of hoodoo. They are placed in Mojo bags, candles, and honey jars, just about anything you will be working on. It is important that you know how to write one. Always make sure your statement of intent is clear. I can't stress enough how important this is. You don't want the spirits to be confused when they are trying to help you succeed in your work. Your higher power will bring you what you are asking for it doesn't matter if it is good for you or not. You make a request and pray for it to happen and it will. So be careful of what you are asking for, make yourself very clear on what it is you want to bring into your life. Sometimes things are easy to get into and hard to get out of. So it's better to be safe than sorry.

LAYING DOWN TRICKS

*T*he laying of tricks is a big part of Conjure. You can lay a trick anywhere the person will walk or place the powder or oil on anything they will touch. You can place the oil on the bottom of their shoe's or place oil on their sox or under clothes. The trick is to name the person the trick is meant for and to pray your petition. I have read that people believe you have to turn around and other stuff to make it work. That's not true! I have used this type of Conjure many times over the years. I have also read where you need to make an X with the powder, this is also not true; I use a line and it works just fine or I will make a cross that has the same effect. I have rubbed oil's on the bottom of shoes by making 3 crosses and praying my petition to what I wanted to happen. One time I set a trick by placing three lines of power in a person's drive way next to their car. A lot of what you find now day's is a bunch of new age crap. I don't think in the old day's people had a lot of time to work on tricks and such. I know my family worked in the tobacco field's from dawn till dusk Monday- Friday and Saturday a half a day. They used what was on hand. Now back to laying tricks. I'll give a few examples; one with powder and another trick using oil made for the right intent.

Let's say I wanted to cause confusion in someone's home. Maybe to hide something one of them was doing.

1. I would make a powder up using either rice powder or dirt from their yard as my base
2. To this I would add:
   Dirt Daubers Nest
   Red Pepper
   Black Mustard Seeds

3. You have to make sure to pray your petition into your ingredients

You can't just mix a bunch of stuff together and expect it to work.

4. When the powder is ready then go to their home and sprinkle it where they will walk in it
5. You need to pray your petition as you are putting the powder down

That's it! It's a done deal. No Hocus Pocus!

If you want to make someone return your love; you can make yourself some Love Oil with:

Jezebel Root
Master of the Woods
Loveage
Magnet
Calamus

I use Fractionated Coconut Oil as base oil for all my oils.

1. Gather your ingredients and pray your petition into them
2. Then place them in the bottle and fill the bottle with your base oil
3. Pray your petition into the bottle the close the bottle up

You now have a Love Oil you can dress the items that your target will come in contact with.

OTHER RESOURCES

Along with Orion Foxwood, Auntie Sindy Todo and Susan Diamond, I am a part of the annual Conjure Con Festival in Santa Cruz, where we provide hands-on workshops on various conjure techniques. You can find out more at ConjureCon.com.

The Lucky Mojo Curio Company, founded by Catherine Yronwode, is one of the largest purveyors of hoodoo, conjure and root-work information and materials in the world. It is major resource and can be accessed through LuckyMojo.com.

Priestess Miriam of the Voodoo Spiritual Temple in New Orleans LA is a deeply loved and respected Voodoo Mambo, and an educational resource on the syncretic nature and sacred practices of American Voodoo. Her temple and educational center is an invaluable resource. More information on Priestess Miriam and her temple can be found at VoodooSpiritualTemple.org.

When visiting New Orleans, one of the most resourceful and informed historians, tour guides, and New Orleans Voodoo Mambos you will find is Mary Milan, also known as Bloody Mary of Bloody Mary's Tours. For information on Mary and her tours, see BloodyMarysTours.com.

You can find out more about my dear friend Orion Foxwood and his Appalachian Southern Conjure at his website OrionFoxwood.com.

And of course, you can check out my products and services at my own website, OldStyleConjure.com.

INDEX

A

B

C

D

G

H

J

K

L

Licorice, 150, 196, 252, 255, 265-266

Light Bringer, 7, 95

Lightening Water, 223

Lightning, 82, 88-89, 155-156, 158

Load, 50, 62, 134, 162, 172, 175, 258, 263, 265

Lock, 77, 85-86, 116, 148, 150, 155

Lodestone, 120, 152, 196, 201, 235-236, 251, 265

Lodestone Grit, 120, 196, 201

Lodestones, 251

Lord God, 137

Lot, 16-17, 33, 35, 54, 66, 73, 78, 95, 97-98, 111, 117, 131, 135, 140-141, 143, 145-146, 159, 169-170, 183, 188, 190, 205, 213, 218, 229, 231, 257-258, 264, 271, 273

Lovage, 58, 61

Love, 8-9, 12, 20, 22, 57, 59-62, 81-82, 87, 90, 97, 108, 119-120, 143, 145, 156, 163, 170, 174, 176, 178, 183, 187, 196, 201, 205, 207, 209, 218, 226, 229, 242, 247, 249, 251, 257, 262, 265, 270-271, 274

Love Conjure, 9, 57, 265

Love Conjure Doll, 9, 265

Love Drawing Bag, 187

Love Drawing Powder, 201

Love Me Oil, 196

Love Oil, 274

Love Work Use, 120

Loveage Root, 87, 156, 196

Lover, 87, 145, 152

Lucky Mojo Curio Company, 277

LuckyMojo, 277

Lucy, 7, 95-100

M

Magic, 11-12, 15, 17-18, 146, 164, 217, 251, 259-260

Magnet, 58, 60, 66-67, 72, 87, 96, 150, 156, 158, 160-161, 172-173, 177, 180, 187, 192, 228, 251, 260, 274

Mama, 12, 16-17, 63, 108-109, 143, 159, 169, 175, 193-194, 200, 209, 213, 233-234, 245-246

Mama Starr, 12

Mammy, 26

Man, 33, 40, 44-45, 51, 80-82, 84, 95, 144, 146, 158, 213, 215,

247, 265

Marjoram, 222, 228

Marriage, 119, 156, 176, 206, 231-232

Marriage Lamp, 176

Martyr, 103

Master Root, 173, 237

Matthew, 123

Medicine Bottle, 48, 51, 58-59, 65, 85-86, 150, 152-153, 202

Medicine Bottles, 8, 153

Mercury, 122-123, 192

Mexican, 164

N

S

T

U

V

W

Y

Z

ABOUT THE AUTHOR

STARR CASAS

I am an ol' Kentucky-born traditional Old Style Conjure woman who works with herbs, roots, and the Spirits. I am also known as a two headed root doctor and spiritual advisor. I learned how to do this work from my momma and grandmomma, who in turn, learned from their elders. Apart from my elders, I had wonderful folks coming into my life, who taught me hands on spiritual work.

Conjure, or what people now call Hoodoo, has always been around. In my family we didn't call it Hoodoo. We simply knew this to be "Conjure" or "work."

I have been a Conjure woman for over 50 years. I first learned how to read playing cards at 16, and by the time I was 17, I was already doing spiritual cleansings, or what some call uncrossing work, as well as healing work. At first I limited my work to the family, but when I turned 25, I knew it was time to start helping others. I began to do Conjure work full time for folks that were referred to me by my relatives or by others who knew me. I always worked only by word of mouth until three years ago, when I felt it was time to share my gift of Conjure work on the Internet.

I serve my community at my little shop where I offer consultations for those seeking help from a caring and compassionate spiritual worker. I also offer candle burning services to set a vigil light on troubles and concerns. I offer Conjure mini courses, as well as Old Style Conjure Oils, Conjure hands (mojo bags), Hoodoo prayer kits, Conjure bottles, and Conjure dollies to give power and domination. All of my products are blessed and prayed over by me to give clients the upper hand in all situations, to master their troubles and come out victorious, to be the leader that God wants them to be.

You can contact me at:

Website: OldStyleConjure.com
Blog: OldStyleConjure.blogspot.com
Blog   Radio: BlogTalkRadio.com/OldStyleConjure
Etsy: Etsy.com/shop/OldStyleConjure

PENDRAIG   PENDRAIG

Magickal Works
From Pendraig Publishing

Balkan Traditional Witchcraft
Radomir Ristic

Buckland's Domino Divinaton
Fortune-Telling with Dóminös
and the Games of Dóminös
Raymond Buckland

Buckland's Practical Color Magick
Raymond Buckland

Hedge-Rider
Witches and the Underworld
Eric De Vries

Magical Rites from the Crystal Well
The Classic Book for Witches and Pagans
Ed Fitch

Masks of the Muse
Building a relationship
with the Goddess of the West
Veronica Cummer

Mastering the Mystical Heptarchy
Scott Stenwick

Scottish Herbs and Fairy Lore
Ellen Evert Hopman

Enchantment
The Witch's Art of Manipulation by
Gesture, Gaze and Glamour
Peter Paddon

Sorgitzak: Old Forest Craft
*Stories and messages
from the gods of Old Europe*
Veronica Cummer

Dancing the Blood
Sorgitzak II
Veronica Cummer

Sybil Leek:
Out of the Shadows
Christine Jones

The Crooked Path
*Selected Transcripts from
the Crooked Path Podcast*
Peter Paddon

The Flaming Circle
*A Reconstruction of the
Old Ways of Britain and Ireland*
Robin Artisson

The Forge of Tubal Cain
*Southern California Witchcraft,
Roebuck, and the Clan of Tubal Cain*
Ann Finnin

The Horn of Evenwood
Robin Artisson

The Resurrection of the Meadow
Robin Artisson

To Fly By Night
An Anthology of Hedgewitchery
Veronica Cummer

Visceral Magick
*Bridging the Gap
Between Magic and Mundane*
Peter Paddon

Witching Way of the Hollow Hill
*The Gramarye of the Folk
Who Dwell Below the Mound*
Robin Artisson

CPSIA information can be obtained
at www.ICGtesting.com
Printed in the USA
LVOW10s1229020717

540116LV00010B/716/P

9 781936 922567